WITHDRAWN

W9-ADX-638

Riveting and Rationing in Dixie

Riveting and Rationing in Dixie

ALABAMA WOMEN
AND THE SECOND WORLD WAR

Mary Martha Thomas

THE UNIVERSITY OF ALABAMA PRESS

Tuscaloosa and London

WITHDRAWN

Copyright © 1987 by
The University of Alabama Press
Tuscaloosa, Alabama 35487
All rights reserved
Manufactured in the United States of America

Library of Congress Cataloging-in-Publication Data

Thomas, Mary Martha, 1927–
  Riveting and rationing in Dixie.

  Bibliography: p.
  Includes index.
  1. World War, 1939–1945—Women—Alabama. 2. Women—
Employment—Alabama—History—20th century. 3. World
War, 1939–1945—Economic aspects—Alabama. 4. Alabama—
Social conditions. I. Title.
D810.W7T46   1987   940.53′15′04209761   86-16068
ISBN 0-8173-0329-4 (alk. paper)

British Library Cataloguing-in-Publication Data is available.

For Philip

DC 89111DO: 750077

Contents

Acknowledgments

While working on this book, I have accumulated many debts that I cannot begin to repay. I thank all who have helped me.

The initial research was funded in part by one of the first faculty research grants established by Jacksonville State University in 1982. This grant made possible a trip to the National Archives in Washington, D.C., where Jerry Hess aided me in locating the material on Alabama in the records of the various government agencies. At the Alabama Department of Archives and History, I am especially indebted to Jean Rankin, who provided me with much assistance finding state sources. Caldwell Delany at the City of Mobile Museum graciously allowed me unlimited access to the holdings of the museum. I also appreciate the assistance of Jane Keaton at the Department of Archives of the Birmingham Public Library.

Susan Hartmann of Ohio State University offered invaluable insights and positive suggestions to improve the manuscript. I deeply appreciate her careful reading and criticism. Several colleagues at Jacksonville State University consented to read and sometimes re-read my manuscript. I owe a debt of gratitude especially to Ronald Caldwell, who helped me focus my writing and suggested the title for the book. I am also indebted to Anne Johnson, Lee Gilbert, Grace Gates, and George Whitesel, who gave freely of their time and made many helpful suggestions. Michael Thomason of the University of South Alabama assisted me in locating and photographing the pictures included in the book.

Gordon Thomas, my son, insisted that I could and should learn to use a word processor to facilitate the writing. It took a lot of convincing, but now I am a strong advocate of word processing. Philip Thomas, my husband, graciously listened to endless discussions about what I had found and how I was trying to put it all together. He consented to his life being rearranged to fit a research or a writing schedule. For all of this help I am most grateful.

Riveting and Rationing in Dixie

Introduction

World War II profoundly changed the old order of American society and economy and presented women with opportunities for new and expanded roles in the life of the nation. As the selective service drafted men into the armed forces, a tremendous labor shortage developed, both in the rapidly expanding defense industries and in the private sector. The government then turned to "womanpower" and encouraged women to take paid wartime jobs, enlist in the military, become nurses, or perform volunteer work. Thousands of Alabama women responded by taking jobs in the airplane plants, the shipyards, and the munition depots of the state. A few women contributed to the war effort by joining the newly created WACS or WAVES. Other women volunteered their services to roll bandages, spot airplanes, issue ration books, or act as nurses' aides. Instead of the usual wife, mother, and homemaker role, Alabama women were asked to undertake a wide variety of unusual tasks. The most important change for women was their employment in jobs normally occupied by men, positions that paid higher wages than those in traditionally female fields and were thought to require "masculine" abilities and attitudes. The ability of women to step into men's shoes and wear them rather comfortably posed an implicit challenge to traditional notions about femininity and female limitations. The war, then, had the potential of drastically changing society and the position of women because of its duration and the extent of female participation, which necessitated a dramatic reassessment of women's role in American life.

Scholars disagree over the long-term impact of the war on women's role in American life and over whether the war period should be characterized as a time of continuity or of dramatic change in definitions of women's place. At one end of the spectrum is William H. Chafe, who published a pathbreaking book in 1972 on women in the twentieth century. Chafe saw the war as a watershed in enlarging women's role by promoting new patterns of behavior and ideas about what women could and could not do. He recognized that economic equality remained a distant goal, but he believed the content of women's lives had changed and an important new area of potential activity had opened up to them.[1] Soon after Chafe's pioneering work, other historians looked at the events in greater detail and came to different conclusions.

Leila Rupp, Karen Anderson, and Eleanor Straub all saw continuity rather than change in women's roles; they believe continuity was upheld by the power of social controls. Based on an analysis of German and American propaganda from 1939 to 1945, Rupp identified several ways portrayals of war workers simultaneously urged the acceptance of women in male jobs and preserved feminine identities. These ranged from comparing factory work to housework to using war workers as sex objects. She concluded that the emergency did not cause fundamental changes in attitudes toward women.[2] Anderson believed that the war made acceptable the notion that women could combine home roles and paid employment, but that despite the temporary gains of the war years, women's status within the labor force was scarcely better than it had been previously.[3] Straub discussed the exclusion of women from policy making in the War Manpower Commission (WMC). She found that the chairman of the WMC reluctantly appointed a Women's Advisory Committee and then refused to give its members a vote or listen to their advice.[4]

D'Ann Campbell also stressed continuity, but she believed that it was rooted in women's satisfaction with their status. She described the experience not only of working women but also of women in the military, in nursing, in volunteer work, and in the home. Women's major goal during the war years was to protect and enrich their private spheres. Campbell concluded that they remained concerned primarily with their homes and families.[5]

Susan Hartmann, however, believed that the effect of the war was mixed and that sweeping generalizations about war and social change are difficult to make. The war had no uniform effect on women; some women benefited, others did not. Despite its potential for changing sex roles, she found that the war also contained powerful forces that checked women's aspirations. But at the same time, she identified the seeds of change, especially in the lives of individual women who left their homes to take on outside jobs.[6] These recent historians have shown that there was a high degree of continuity in women's roles during the 1940s and that the conservative postwar views of women were rooted in economic, social, and ideological structures that transcended the brief wartime campaign to alter gender roles.

My purpose in this study is to explore the wartime experiences of Alabama women. First I will describe women who worked in the defense industries—how they were recruited and trained, where they worked, under what conditions they worked, and what changes employers made to accommodate them. Next I will relate the experiences of volunteer women—their role in the Ground Observer Corps, the Citizens' Service Corps, the Red Cross, and other volunteer agencies. Then I will consider the role of the housewife and how she coped with homemaking during a time of rationing, housing shortages, lack of schools, and inadequate medical facilities. In the context of all of these topics, I will also describe the changes in the society and the economy of the state during these years. Finally, I will address the issue of how these wartime experiences affected the perception of women and women's place in the society and the economy. Were the war years a time of change or did the forces of continuity prevail?

CHAPTER 1

Home Fronts: The

Nation and Alabama

World War II created conditions that required women in Alabama and throughout the nation to take on a variety of new roles. The state and federal governments conducted numerous recruitment campaigns encouraging women to take jobs in the defense industries, enlist in the armed forces, or contribute their time to volunteer work. The women of the state responded by enlisting in the WACS, WAVES, or Nurse Corps; by taking jobs in airplane modification plants, shipyards, and ordnance depots; by working in offices or service industries; or by volunteering to learn first aid, work in war bond drives, or cooperate in blackout drills. Only a very small number joined the armed forces or the Nurse Corps; hence the basic decision Alabama women made involved some combination of volunteer activity, paid jobs in war industries, and unpaid work at home. The demands of wartime encouraged Alabama women to change their traditional role from one of wife, mother, and homemaker to that of war worker.

Nationwide the media image of women changed as an increasing number sought and accepted jobs in defense plants, offices, and service industries. The most highly publicized role for women was that of defense worker. As millions of men joined the armed forces, tremendous labor shortages occurred in the nation's defense industries. The federal government, industry, the media, and women's clubs joined in urging women to do their patriotic duty by taking jobs to help the war effort. By 1943 the reserve of single women had been exhausted, and recruitment was aimed more directly at married women. As a result, more than 8 million women nationwide entered the work force during the war. The overall participation rate of women jumped from 25 percent in 1940 to 36 percent in 1945, an increase greater than that of the preceding four decades.[1]

The extent to which World War II altered women's lives can be fully understood only with reference to the crisis of the nationwide Depression that preceded it. In 1933 some 12 to 15 million Americans were unemployed, 25 percent of the work force; by 1939 unemployment still stood at 10 million. During the 1930s, the federal government joined with local governments, school boards, and private businesses to exclude married women from the work force. Twenty-six states considered laws prohibiting employment of married women. The majority of the nation's public schools, over 40 percent of public utilities, and more than 10 percent of American department stores enforced a curb on the employment of wives. Society condemned wives who worked outside the home as selfish, greedy women who took jobs away from male breadwinners. A Gallup poll in 1936 reported that 82 percent of the respondents believed that women with employed husbands should not work outside the home.[2] In the Great Depression, Americans strongly promoted male employment and severely criticized female employment.

Despite the cultural and legal restraints, however, the Depression failed to reverse general, long-term trends nationwide in women's employment. Their participation in the labor force grew from 22 to 25 percent during the decade of the 1930s, and the proportion of married women who were employed increased. These changes were consistent in direction, if not in rate, with trends that had been under way since 1900. The bulk of the married women who worked, however, were in desperate financial straits and were members of ethnic and racial minorities. The white, middle-class, educated women who pursued professional careers remained overwhelmingly single; for them the roles of worker and homemaker remained separate.[3]

The experience of Alabama women deviated from that of women nationally. Instead of female employment continuing a slow, steady increase, the percent of Alabama women in the labor force declined from 27 in 1930 to 24 in 1940. White women continued to participate in about the same numbers, but black women suffered a decline in employment during the Depression. Approximately 17 percent of all white women were in the labor force in both 1930 and 1940, but the percent of black women declined from 44 in 1930 to 34 in 1940.[4] Most of the black women who dropped out of the labor force during the 1930s were probably discouraged workers who could not find jobs and gave up looking.

Black and white women lived in two separate worlds in Alabama in the prewar years. Relatively few white women were employed outside the home, whereas almost half of all black women sought paying jobs. White women worked only for a few years until they married, then they dropped out of the job market. It was not socially acceptable for a white married woman to work. Only white women who were single, widowed, divorced, or whose husbands could not provide adequate support for them took jobs. Black women had little choice in the matter; they had to support themselves or others. Even employed white women worked at totally different jobs than did black women. About a fourth of all white women in 1940 worked in clerical or sales jobs; another fourth worked in factories (textile factories were large employers of women); and 17 percent were employed as professionals (most of these were public school teachers). In contrast, more than half of all black women worked as domestics, and the next largest category (17 percent) worked as agricultural laborers.[5] These women desperately needed employment and would seek wartime jobs.

The hesitancy to employ women changed drastically during the war. By 1943 the War Manpower Commission encouraged women to work in defense plants and government offices and pressured employers to tap the vast resources of womanpower. "Almost overnight," wrote Mary Anderson of the Women's Bureau of the Department of Labor, "women were classified from a marginal to a basic labor supply." Women were told that they were ideally suited physically and mentally for war work. A special bulletin produced by the Women's Bureau made the following claim: "Women excel in work requiring care and constant alertness, good eyesight, and use of light instruments . . . work calling for little physical exertion. . . . Women excel at work requiring manipulative dexterity and speed, but which permits the individual to set her own tempo and work in a sitting position."[6]

Journalists and the media glorified the "Jane Who Made the Planes" as well as the famous "Rosie the Riveter," whose peroxide curls were tied for safety in a fashionable snood. Defense plants absorbed 2 million female workers to make airplane frames, parachutes, life rafts, munitions, gas masks, and electrical equipment. They assembled machine guns, operated hand drills, cleaned spark plugs, loaded shells, and wired instrument panels—and they learned their jobs in two to six months. Women could be found in such novel places as on the docks, in the steel mills, in shipyards, and in aircraft assembly plants.[7]

Their invasion of the shipyards was especially dramatic. In 1939, only thirty-six women in the United States worked in shipyards. Most yards did not employ women even in their offices. By 1943 women made up 4 percent of shipyard employees and by the end of the war, nearly 10 percent. The aircraft industry adapted even more rapidly to female labor. A study by the Women's Bureau showed that a third of aircraft jobs could be done by women. By the middle of the war, female employment in engine plants peaked at 31 percent and in some tasks women made up as much as 71 percent of the work force.[8]

These national changes were reflected in events in Alabama. Most Alabama women in defense industries were employed in airplane modification and repair plants. Recruitment drives were held in Mobile to encourage women to work at the Mobile Air Service Command (MoASC), where they eventually accounted for almost half of the employees. They made up 40 percent of the Bechtel-McCone-Parsons plant in Birmingham. Ordnance depots also hired large numbers of female workers. The percent of women employed at the Alabama Ordnance Works at Childersburg was as high as 48; at the same time at the Redstone Arsenal and the Huntsville Arsenal women made up between 25 and 35 percent of the work force. Textile mills also had war contracts, and they continued their prewar dependence on female labor, varying from 40 to 70 percent. Heavy industries such as iron and steel and shipbuilding used women in much smaller numbers. The Mobile shipyards employed approximately 10 percent women. These "lady welders," however, received publicity out of proportion to their numbers. Women also found substantial employment at the various military bases, Fort McClellan in Anniston, Maxwell Air Force base in Montgomery, and smaller camps throughout the state. Hence many Alabama women followed in the footsteps of the famous Rosie the Riveter by assuming unaccustomed roles in wartime industries.[9]

Before turning to a detailed description of women war workers in Alabama, it is necessary to describe some of the economic and social developments in the state that were a consequence of wartime growth. Alabama, like other states in the nation, experienced far-reaching changes in its society and economy as a result of World War II.

Alabama received its share of war industries, which revived the Depression economy and essentially brought full employment by 1943.[10] Birmingham, the leading industrial city in the state, had millions of dollars of War Production Board contracts. Plants that once made women's underwear now turned out shell belts. Others that had manufactured metal lawn furniture now made hospital beds and bomb racks. A plant that formerly rolled out cotton gins now sped ship machinery off the assembly line. An awning company made army tents. Airplane and tank parts were the products of a former cast-iron pipe manufacturer. More than 85 percent of Birmingham's industries were engaged in war production. In addition, the mills of the iron and steel industry shifted from peacetime to wartime pro-

duction. The Tennessee Coal and Iron Company (TCI), whose pay-
roll was the lifeblood of Birmingham, received large war orders. A
new blast furnace, which was completed in April 1942, increased
production by 17 percent. TCI produced its one millionth shell as
early as November 1942. Plates rolled from a new TCI plate mill in
May 1942, which added 50 percent to the company's plate-producing
capacity. The Ingalls Iron Works Company fabricated steel for the
shipyards of the Gulf. Whole sections of liberty ships were welded
together and transported overnight to the Ingalls Shipbuilding Company in Pascagoula, Mississippi.[11]

The next largest industrial center in the state was Gadsden, where
Republic Steel Corporation and Goodyear Tire and Rubber Company both had operations. The Goodyear plant had been established
in 1929. Republic Steel bought out Gulf States Steel Company in
1937 and immediately increased production by 50 percent. By 1943
Republic was manufacturing pig iron, steel ingots, billets and slams,
merchant bar steel, concrete reinforcing steel angles, and plates for
shipbuilding.[12] Other iron and steel plants in the state were the
Kilby Steel Company in Anniston and Decatur Iron and Steel Company in Decatur.[13]

Shipyards mushroomed along the Gulf Coast and even at some
inland ports. The Maritime Commission, a civilian agency, sponsored new or greatly enlarged shipyards in several ports in 1940,
one of which was Mobile. Because of its connections with the iron
and steel industry of Birmingham, as well as its long tradition of
shipbuilding, Mobile quickly became a major wartime port, where
ships were completed in record numbers. The Alabama Dry Dock
and Shipbuilding Company (ADDSCO) launched a new 16,000-ton
dry dock, which, together with previous facilities, enabled the company to construct 102 tankers and 20 liberty ships and to repair more
than 2,800 additional vessels during the war years. The Gulf Shipbuilding Company, which opened on the old Chickasaw yard site,
produced 29 minesweepers, 30 tankers, 7 destroyers, and a landing
dock. The Waterman Repair Division completely reoutfitted 50 vessels and made repairs on other craft.[14] The number of ADDSCO

employees increased from less than 2,000 in 1940 to approximately 30,000 by 1943 and that of Gulf Shipbuilding from 240 to 11,600.[15] Even in inland Decatur ships were manufactured at the yards of the Ingalls Shipbuilding Corporation, which specialized in all-welded cargo ships.[16]

In addition to the shipyards, aircraft plants were developed in a line across the South from the Dallas–Fort Worth area to Marietta, Georgia. An important airplane modification plant was established along this line at Birmingham by the Bechtel-McCone-Parsons Company. The plant was built in sixty-one days between January 15 and March 19, 1943, at a cost of $15 million. The Birmingham site was selected over twenty-four others, a choice that caused great rejoicing in the city. This ultramodern modification center was erected on 260 acres west of the municipal airport where a year earlier only grass and weeds flourished. Liberty bombers were flown in from Detroit, Fort Worth, and Tulsa to be modified to the specifications of the air force by installing secret radio equipment and navigational instruments, adjusting gun turrets and guns, and protecting the engines against moisture and cold.[17] Bechtel-McCone-Parsons employed large numbers of women for these tasks.

War production spurred new developments in chemical manufacture and related processes. By early 1942 the southern landscape was dotted with ordnance plants that made smokeless powder and other explosives from cotton linters, wood cellulose, and petroleum products. Every southern state participated but the largest plant was the DuPont Alabama Ordnance Works at Childersburg, near Birmingham. With the building of the $70 million plant beginning in January 1941, Childersburg became the powder keg of Alabama, an arsenal of the Southland.[18] Connected with the DuPont plant was the Brecon Loading Company, a much smaller organization that loaded artillery charges in bags. A second major munitions center was located in Huntsville with the Redstone Arsenal and the Huntsville Arsenal. Redstone was constructed on a site ten miles out of Huntsville that earlier was devoted to raising peanuts and cotton. This shell-loading plant as well as the Huntsville Arsenal, which produced toxic gas, employed a large number of civilians, many of whom were women. Women also found employment at the Childersburg operations.[19]

Important growth also occurred in nonferrous metals. Robert S. Reynolds of ALCOA secured loans from the Reconstruction Finance Corporation (RFC) to establish an aluminum plant at Listerhill, near Muscle Shoals. This plant—an open-hearth oil-fired remelt furnace—was the largest of its type in the country, producing 120 million pounds of aluminum a year. In 1939 ALCOA expanded production in the South by establishing a plant at Mobile. This growing industry was vital in the production of airplanes.[20]

Other obvious evidence of Alabama's war activity was the growth of military establishments. Alabama had long been an important military center, but shortly after the war began the older bases increased in size and many new ones were created. As early as 1940, the army air corps built a major base in Mobile at Brookley Field on the bay south of the city. This construction marked the beginning of a wartime economy that was to transform Mobile. Established originally as a center for airplane modification, especially B-24 bombers, it also served as a major depot for military equipment because of Mobile's deep harbor. By 1943 Brookley's civilian work force approached 17,000 people, half of whom were women. Additional thousands of air corps personnel poured in from the entire country. Other air force facilities included Maxwell Field at Montgomery, which was the Southeast Army Air Forces Training Center, Craig Field, a smaller training center near Selma, and Courtland Air Base, an Army Air Forces Basic Flying School, twenty miles from Decatur. The army greatly expanded Fort McClellan near Anniston, the Anniston Army Depot, Fort Rucker near Dothan, and Camp Sibert, a smaller camp for training near Gadsden.[21]

In addition to increasing the industrial capacity of Alabama, the wartime growth also brought other changes. The area developed a pool of skilled workers, experienced managers, and some local capital. Perhaps more important than physical assets were intangible benefits such as demonstration of industrial potential, new habits of mind, and a recognition that industrialization demanded community services. Alabama acquired certain essential ingredients for an economic takeoff.[22]

Many of these economic developments were acquired, however, at a heavy cost of social dislocation. The governor of Alabama, Chauncey Sparks, described the social conditions in the state in *War Comes to Alabama,* published in 1943 by the Bureau of Public Administration at the University of Alabama. Governor Sparks believed that the rapid industrialization and the demand for labor created problems which government did not have the resources to handle. Migration into and within the state complicated these problems. Shack, trailer, and tent cities were erected to house war workers. Sparks wrote: "In such communities are found constant and serious threats to health, while the problems of welfare are varied and never ending. Schools, too, have become a serious problem there, with the demands for school services far out running local ability to supply teachers, equipment, and plants. The present 'boom' is not without its seamy side, particularly as regards human welfare."[23]

As early as May 1942 war migrants were becoming a problem for many southern towns. They were sometimes described as new "Okies"—not the Okies of John Steinbeck and the Depression but industrial workers, often skilled craftsmen, drawn to war-booming ports and inland production centers by the promise of ready employment and high wages. The problems of industrial migration were sufficiently severe for a committee of the U.S. House of Representatives to launch an investigation. On May 7–8, 1942, this committee conducted hearings in Huntsville. Among the topics discussed were migration to and from farms, the movement of labor to and between war industries, the effect of wartime demands and priorities, and the effect on living conditions of the influx of workers to key centers. The witnesses came primarily from the Huntsville area but included representatives from the entire state. The consensus was that if war production were to reach its full potential, migration must be stabilized and controlled. The call for married women who were residents of war production areas to take jobs was largely a way of limiting the migration to defense centers.[24]

Governor Sparks did not name a specific location in his essay, but his remarks obviously described social conditions in Mobile. Few American cities experienced the violent, sweeping changes caused by World War II that Mobile did. In 1940 Mobile was essentially a moderate-sized southern town with a history dating back to an early eighteenth-century settlement by the French. A physically beautiful city with convenient access to the bay, it held an annual Mardi Gras, a heritage from its Roman Catholic tradition, and enjoyed a leisurely paced life. But the experiences of the war drastically altered its population and social institutions and forcefully shaped its future. The most obvious change was the influx of thousands of people starved by the Depression who streamed into the city in search of defense jobs. Coming largely from the impoverished farms and towns of rural Alabama, Mississippi, Georgia, and west Florida, they swelled the population of the metropolitan area from 114,906 in 1940 to 201,369 in 1944.[25] To the farmers of this area, who had suffered from an economic depression since 1919, Mobile with job opportunities seemed a mecca. Woefully unprepared to deal with this 75 percent increase in population, the Mobile area struggled to provide basic services. The county led the list of the ten most congested areas in the United States.[26]

Living conditions were chaotic during the war; newly arrived workers could not find adequate housing, transportation, medical services, educational facilities, or food supply. Even as early as mid-1942, less than a year after war was declared, Mobilians found that their city had been transformed and their pattern of living changed. By September 1942 retail and wholesale trade had doubled, industrial employment had increased three times, daily phone calls had tripled, and newspaper circulation was up one and a half times.[27]

As a result of the stress placed on community institutions and social services by the influx of war workers, an angry chasm developed between the migrants and the older residents. Native Mobilians saw their world being destroyed by newcomers whom they considered primitive, uneducated, backwoods people. One Mobilian expressed common feelings: "We are quite exercised about the problems these newcomers raise for the city. . . . Juvenile delinquency, illegitimate babies, venereal disease. . . . They are what we call riffraff." A Mobile teacher described the newcomers as "the lowest type of poor whites, these workers flocking in from the backwoods. They prefer to live in shacks and go barefoot. . . . Give them a good home and they wouldn't know what to do with it. They . . . let their kids run wild on the streets. I only hope we can get rid of them after the war."[28]

Such resentment was the product of the clash of values and interests between the urban middle class, many of whom were still living on the memories of the glory days of the antebellum cotton trade, and workers from a background of rural poverty who were seeking an opportunity to earn a living wage. War workers found Mobile a closed society that resented all newcomers and offered little cooperation in making their lives more comfortable. The cleavage between the two groups was so severe that the president of the Chamber of Commerce, R. D. Hayes, made a plea for a friendlier attitude and cooperation between natives and newcomers. Mobilians commonly saw the newcomers as responsible for the problems the city faced and were unwilling to recognize that the war was transforming society everywhere. Despite the wish that the newcomers would leave when the war was over, many stayed and became permanent residents.[29]

Other Alabama cities also witnessed increasing population, housing shortages, crowding in the schools, and a lack of medical facilities, but their problems pale in comparison to those of Mobile. Birmingham's population increased from 267,583 in 1940 to 303,000 in 1943, a modest 13 percent, and the greater Birmingham area population increased by only 17 percent. By comparison, the population of the Mobile area increased by 75 percent. The population growth was also reflected in the number of those gainfully employed. Employment increased 28.6 percent, from 139,123 in 1940 to 178,873 in

1943. Increased employment also meant increased payrolls. In 1940 weekly payrolls were $2.7 million; by 1943 they were $4.2 million, an increase of 55.5 percent.[30] These figures add up to boom times because the newly prosperous war worker was eager to spend the new earnings.

Birmingham's shift from peacetime industry to wartime production was accomplished with a minimum of social dislocation and turmoil. The city was large enough and its social services sufficiently well developed to absorb the excess population in housing, schools, hospitals, and transportation. Hence Birmingham was able to accommodate the newcomers without the trauma that Mobile experienced. Sometimes the streets were more crowded than usual and lines often formed for many purposes—waiting for a bus, applying for a job, a "B" gasoline ration book, an automobile tag, a movie ticket, or even a marriage license. Men and women simply learned to accept crowded conditions and long lines.

Virginia Van Der Veer, a young newspaper reporter, summed up her description of wartime Birmingham in these words: "Work, sorrow, loneliness, and courage are the fortunes of war for those who fight at home. War comes and lives with us. It is a powerful magnet compelling, controlling, pulling onward millions of . . . humans. In a year and two months, the magnet has drawn all men, women, and children in this country out of their accustomed private paths onto one broad crowded highway. . . . We are rich. Above all other nations, the United States is well-fed, amply provided for. . . . Industrially, physically, socially—war has not been too hard on Birmingham."[31]

The small town of Childersburg, southeast of Birmingham, had the potential to be more affected by the war in proportion to its size than even Mobile. Just north of Childersburg was the Alabama Ordnance Works built by the DuPont Corporation, which produced smokeless powder, TNT, and Tetryl. Some 14,000 people were employed in the area, although at the height of construction the total was as high as 21,000. In 1940 Childersburg was a town of only 500 with no paved streets, no hotel, and no vacant houses because most people were born and died in the same house. By 1942 its population had increased to 6,000 which caused near chaos.[32]

Because these small communities did not have an adequate labor supply for the ordnance plant, most workers commuted from Birmingham. The trip entailed a drive of thirty-nine miles along a "suicide strip" where accidents were frequent. The inauguration of a shuttle train between the city and the plant, as well as the operation of buses, reduced the number of cars at the ordnance parking lots to about nine thousand a day. Cars passed the intersection of the access road and the highway at the rate of one every seven seconds throughout the twenty-four hours; traffic was bumper-to-bumper whenever shifts changed. Four state highway patrolmen were assigned full time to Childersburg while six more on motorcycles handled the flow of traffic out of Birmingham.[33]

By the end of 1942, the situation began to improve slightly. A new access road to the plant had been constructed, which lessened traffic congestion, as did the paving of the main street. A new water and sewage system provided water for homes on the hill. A United Service Organization (USO) center operated twenty-four hours a day; a federal housing project was home for several hundred workers; and the services of the Works Progress Administration (WPA) nursery school had been expanded to meet the needs of the female employees of the Brecon Loading Company.[34]

The city of Anniston, sixty-five miles east of Birmingham, experienced substantial growth and changes but little shortage of labor and a minimum of dislocation as a result of wartime expansion. The impact of the war was felt mostly because of the presence of Fort McClellan, a permanent army post located just north of the city. The post inducted all of the state's selective service registrants as well as training thousands of soldiers from all over the nation. In 1943 the fort was an Infantry Replacement Training Center with a capacity of 35,000 troops. It also served as the induction center of the newly organized WACS. Hence, thousands of men and women passed through Anniston during the war. The Anniston Army Depot was built in 1941 and managed by the army until 1943, when a subsidiary of the Chrysler Corporation assumed its management. Virtually all of Anniston's other industries were converted to war production. The Kilby Steel Company made carbon alloy, steel, and shell forgings. The Monsanto Company made aluminum, and several textile mills had government contracts. As a result of these war industries and the presence of a military fort, the population of Anniston increased some 13,000 during the war years, from 25,523 in 1940 to approximately 38,000 by 1943. Housing conditions were tight but not desperate and the labor supply kept pace with the demand. No acute manpower shortage developed.[35]

Directly north of Anniston on the Coosa River was the industrial city of Gadsden, which did experience severe labor shortages. Gadsden's population increased 27 percent, from 36,975 in 1940 to approximately 47,000 in 1943. The backbone of Gadsden's industrial power was the Goodyear Rubber plant and the Republic Steel operation, in addition to a cluster of smaller industries, all of which had defense contracts. The number of employed workers increased nearly four times, from 4,800 before the war to more than 18,000 by 1943. Government contractors stumbled over each other trying to find good help. Service and clerical workers left their low-paying jobs and sought new ones with defense plants, which offered greatly increased pay. Small business establishments had difficulties maintaining workers, a typical case being a café that was forced to post a sign that read, "Will open at 11:00 A.M.—providing we have the help."[36]

Huntsville, in the northern part of the state, also saw substantial growth and began to develop into a major city. In 1940 Huntsville was a small town with a population of 13,171. By 1943, after the construction of the Redstone Arsenal and the Huntsville Arsenal, the population increased to 19 to 20,000. The metropolitan area saw an increase from 30,000 in 1940 to 45,000 by 1943. As early as 1941 the army acquired forty thousand acres of land southwest of the city, where it built and operated an enormous arsenal and ordnance plant. At the peak of construction 13,000 workers were employed at the

Advertisement promoting a 1943 "women-in-war-jobs" recruitment campaign. "If you are in a war job, stay in it," the text of the ad advises women.
"If you are not—then take training for shipyard jobs or other essential war
jobs." (*Mobile Press Register,* February 21, 1943; courtesy of University
of South Alabama Library)

two plants. Once construction was completed by mid-1943, the population decreased because fewer production workers were needed than construction workers. Hence the most severe congestion occurred during the months the plants were being built.[37]

The biggest change in Huntsville was the prosperity brought by the boom economy. Business was good, and cash was plentiful. Most people believed the good times would not last and were inclined to take advantage of the situation. The newcomers in the town were easily assimilated into the community. Unlike Mobile, no feeling existed that these people were undesirable or carpetbaggers. Most newcomers expected to stay only during the boom times and return to their farms when the war was over. Few people realized that the wartime boom would continue and Huntsville would become a major industrial area.[38]

Montgomery, Alabama's capital city, had no large-scale industries engaged in defense production, but the city did feel the effect of the war largely through the growth of Maxwell Field and the presence of offices of wartime agencies. Maxwell Field, established in 1922, grew tremendously during the war years. It was the headquarters of the Southeast Army Air Force Training Center, which controlled sixty training fields. In addition to the training of pilots, Maxwell Field was a storage area for airplanes. Montgomery was also the home of wartime agencies, including the Office of Price Administration (OPA), the Office of Defense Transportation, the Selective Service, and the Civilian Defense Council. The city developed the capability to be a distribution center for the entire Southeast by constructing a giant reconsignment depot. All of these various activities increased the population by approximately 30,000, from 78,184 in 1940 to 108,000 by 1943. The city experienced some shortage of housing, but it never became severe. The U.S. Employment Service (USES) described the city as having a labor surplus, but it was sometimes hard to find. A transportation crisis did develop with the overcrowding of buses during rush hour. Montgomery became the first city to attempt to alleviate the problem by staggering school, office, and store hours. Despite these changes, life in the capital was not substantially disturbed by the war.[39]

Alabama's home-front experience was similar to that of other states that had large, new military bases and defense industries. The most immediate and obvious effect was an increase in economic prosperity that brought a higher standard of living. Alabama, along with other southern states, had suffered severe poverty during the Depression. To people who had grown to maturity in those lean years, the boom of the war years stood in stark contrast. The established industries of the state, such as iron and steel, shipbuilding, and rubber, all obtained lucrative war contracts. Even smaller industries, including textiles, had their share of defense orders. The state also saw the establishment of new defense industries, such as airplane modification plants and ordnance depots. Many Alabamians experienced their first real prosperity with substantial pay checks. Virtually everyone who wanted a job could find one, including women, who had usually been viewed as marginal labor. These marginal workers now were considered necessary to winning the war, and large-scale recruitment drives were held to persuade them to enter the work force.

CHAPTER 2

The Recruitment and

Training of Women

As Alabama women responded to the war, they faced the same choices that all American women did. What could they do to aid the war effort? Should they take defense jobs? Should they volunteer for the Red Cross, the USO, or the war bond drives? Or could they serve their country better by remaining at home and caring for their husbands and children? Their choices might involve some combination of all three. Alabama women did choose to enter the work force in record numbers, especially in Mobile, where labor was critically short in supply. Women who were employed before the war were able to upgrade their jobs and increase their income during these boom years. Women who worked before they were married returned to the work force. Older women with grown children were particularly interested in jobs and often became long-term employees. Some women entered the work force for the first time, encouraged by good pay and patriotic motives. Whatever their reasons or circumstances, women chose to enter the work force in increasing numbers.

To encourage women to enter the work force, recruitment drives were conducted at both the national and state levels. The War Manpower Commission promoted both a national campaign to acquaint the public with the problem and intensive local campaigns in areas short of labor. Active recruitment of women occurred in areas where labor was short and the WMC wanted to mobilize local workers. Importing labor was not practical because areas with insufficient labor invariably had housing shortages as well.

The WMC conducted four nationwide campaigns during the war years. The first campaign, held in December 1942, was addressed to both men and women. A second major campaign began in March 1943, followed by the largest effort yet in September 1943. This campaign sought to recruit women for jobs in essential civilian services, such as offices, stores, restaurants, hospitals, and laundries, rather than in war industries. The last campaign began in March 1944 and was sponsored by the Office of War Information, the War Manpower Commission, and the armed forces. The theme of this joint effort among recruiters of civilian and military womanpower was the government's belief that women knew of the need for their participation but were reluctant to take war jobs.[1]

Local recruitment drives in Alabama were conducted concurrently with these national drives. Newspapers in Mobile and Birmingham carried articles and advertisements encouraging women to aid in the war effort by taking jobs in defense or service industries. The propaganda stressed that the war had to be fought with "telephones and typewriters as well as airplanes and ships." Women were encouraged to take jobs to free men for the armed forces. The regional director of the WMC said that winning the war "will mean the employment of handicapped persons, married women, young students, and older persons who would not normally be engaged in any occupation." In short, recruitment was aimed at marginal workers.[2] In Alabama the only organized and sustained drives to recruit women were conducted in Mobile, where the labor shortage was acute. In the course of the war Mobile officials conducted three drives that roughly corresponded to the national drives, one in October 1942, another in February 1943, and a final one in the spring of 1944.

The U.S. Employment Service conducted the first drive to recruit women for war work in September 1942. The agency hoped to enlist a thousand women between the ages of eighteen and thirty-five to work either in the shipyards or at Brookley Field. By the fall of 1942

the Alabama Dry Docks and Shipbuilding Company and the Gulf
Shipbuilding Company had been building liberty ships and tankers
for well over a year. Working twenty-four hours a day six days a
week, they were having difficulty securing and holding an adequate
supply of labor. ADDSCO estimated that it would need nearly seven
thousand workers in the next six months, and Gulf Shipbuilding put
its estimate at fifteen hundred workers. Brookley Field anticipated
employing twenty-five hundred.[3] The director of the vocational
education program said, "We have scraped the bottom of the barrel
as far as men are concerned and women are going to have to take
over the war industry program."[4]

By this time the WMC had decided that women could do almost
anything in wartime production. Mary Anderson of the Women's
Bureau said: "We nominate for the role of discovery of the year, the
woman worker. Until a short time ago considered in certain quarters
a person of limited usefulness, the woman worker is now being hailed
for her nimble fingers and agile brain, and recommended for almost
all kinds of employment."[5] Suddenly women who had been regarded
as a marginal labor supply were being actively recruited. Despite
the shortage of labor and pressure from the WMC, the shipyards
and other private employers were reluctant to hire women. Much
uncertainty existed about whether women would work and how
effective they would be. The general attitude was that women would
be employed only after all the available male labor had been
exhausted.[6]

Echoing the arguments of the War Manpower Commission, the
local newspapers joined in the drive to recruit women. An editorial
writer for the *Mobile Press Register* observed that wars were no
longer for men only and that women were needed in the war industries. Since one out of every three men would be drafted, the government and industry needed women to take their place. The writer
conceded that thousands of Mobile women lacked the time or the
physical qualifications to work outside the home but encouraged
those who could to aid the war effort. The writer noted that war
work would be profitable for women, a point usually not mentioned

because according to the traditional view women worked only for "pin" money. The editorial concluded with a patriotic appeal to women: "Women investigate today, learn what type of work you may be able to do for America's victory effort." Another editorial even encouraged married women to take war jobs. "It's up to the married women . . . now unless millions of housewives go to work . . . we can't adequately supply as large an army as we hope to by the end of next year."[7] The old prohibition against married women working was temporarily shelved.

In August 1942, the two shipyards began employing untrained and casually selected women. The USES recruited some five hundred women and the companies hired two hundred independently. The shipyards did not provide adequate facilities for women such as proper rest rooms, locker space, first aid, and safety equipment. In short, they made little effort to ease their adjustment into what was definitely a male bastion. By October, more than two hundred women had been discharged on the basis of incompetence. Women were hired as a last resort and fired on the slightest pretext. The shipyards did not attract women in any great numbers. Indeed, considering that virtually no women were employed in any shipyards before 1942, not even in office work, it is surprising that the doors of this exclusive male domain opened at all. By June 1943, 9 percent of the employees in the Mobile shipyards were women. The percentage rose to 10.8 in July and reached a high of 11.6 in November 1944.[8] Approximately half of these women workers at any given time were clerical.

The Mobile Air Service Command at Brookley Field had far more success in employing women than did the shipyards. The air command conducted its own recruitment drive for a thousand women in September 1942 by distributing to thirty-two hundred students at Murphy High School information to be given to their mothers, sisters, and women friends. The major job at MoASC was the repair and maintenance of airplane engines, which required workers to use lathes, buffing machines, reamers, and grit paper. Women were considered desirable for this work because their touch was finer than that of a man. Government propaganda often depicted women as having a special proclivity for tedious, repetitive work whether on the assembly line or in the household. This conviction that women excelled at repetitive jobs requiring finger dexterity and much patience stereotyped them as capable of the least skilled jobs. Women who entered training at MoASC were paid $90 per month; after the training period their salary increased to $125.[9]

The working conditions here were more desirable than in the shipyards. MoASC made substantial efforts to help women adjust to their work and to hold down employee turnover by providing an orientation course and in-service training. Assistance was also offered in housing, transportation, and child care in addition to providing movies, dancing, and an attractive new cafeteria.[10] The air command estimated that by the end of the war more women than men would be employed. This prediction came close to being fulfilled. In January 1942, MoASC employed only twenty-three women, but by September the female employment had risen to twenty-three hundred. By May 1943, the percentage had increased to 42.4 and by November 1944 it had risen to 49 percent.[11]

The War Manpower Commission and USES conducted a much more ambitious drive in Mobile February 23–28, 1943, which coincided with the issuance of War Ration Book Two. This drive was the first held in the Southeast and preceded by a few weeks a major national drive by the WMC in March 1943. The Mobile drive was to be a model for forthcoming campaigns in other areas, so the eyes of the nation were on Mobile. If this drive succeeded, its methods would be tried elsewhere. Burton R. Morley, area director of the WMC, worked closely with Fred Gormley of the USES and with representatives of women's organizations, primarily the Business and Professional Women's Club (BPW), in making plans for the drive.

The BPW chaired the steering committee and called the initial meeting to plan the drive, but from then on Morley and Gormley led the organization of the campaign. The only woman's name mentioned was that of the president of the BPW, and her name was listed at the bottom of a long account in the newspaper. Mobile women conducted the actual registration, but they had no policy-making role in planning this important campaign to recruit women. This disregard for women's participation by the state WMC reflected that of the national WMC, which appointed a Women's Advisory Committee with no power, no vote, and no means of influencing decisions.[12]

At an initial meeting January 22, 1943, at the Battle House Hotel, plans were laid for a citywide registration of women in which they would be asked to fill out a questionnaire describing their work experience, their willingness to accept employment, and their child care responsibilities. Registration booths were set up at all schools and downtown locations during the six-day recruitment period. Merchants assisted by placing booths in stores and by setting up displays in store fronts. Women were asked to register either for volunteer work with the Red Cross or the Civilian Defense Council or for paid full-time employment in service establishments or industries. The USES assured women that they would be placed in the jobs best suited to their ability, personality, temperament, and experience. Not everyone had to be a "lady welder" to solve the employment problem. Women were encouraged to work as clerks, stenographers, waitresses, and sales clerks as well as welders and mechanics. Gormley said the USES "after a long study had reported that it can hardly be said that any occupation is absolutely unsuited for the employment of women. Women have always been able to do any kind of work." This was a remarkable statement considering the hitherto rigid classification of jobs by sex.[13]

The USES encouraged every housewife to ask herself, "Can I be of greater service in my home or in a war plant?" Gormley observed that because of the housing shortage it was ridiculous to bring labor to Mobile as long as there were any idle women there. Women were openly encouraged to find care for their children in a nursery or with an older family member, day nurse, or friend. The USES stressed that lack of experience was no bar to women who were willing to hold jobs. Women should consider such questions as: "How and where can I do something useful in the war effort? Can I make the

TO THE WOMEN OF MOBILE

Uncle Sam Says:

I Need YOU!

There is an acute shortage of workers for both Mobile's War Industries and for Essential Civilian Services. Thousands of new residents have come in and taken up a lot of the slack, but they have not proved to be enough. We Mobilians must pitch in and help to overcome this shortage . . . and at once! Practically all available man-power has been exhausted, so the solving of the problem rests with the women. Uncle Sam, through Mobile's office of the War Manpower Commission is asking that you step up and volunteer to take a job either in a War Industry or in some store, office or other essential civilian business. We do not believe that you Women of Mobile will shirk your responsibility . . . we believe you will rally to the call, now.

WHAT WILL YOUR ANSWER BE?

THE WAR MANPOWER COMMISSION Says:

To the Women of Mobile:

You are needed in the war jobs and in other essential civilian jobs directly aiding the war effort in Mobile NOW. Manpower has been practically exhausted. Housing available at this time will not prevent the bringing into Mobile of the thousands of additional workers required for the shipyards and other war and essential industries. We must depend upon you—each woman-power. There are idle machines in war plants which you can operate. There are idle jobs in the shipyards which you can fill. There are jobs in stores, offices, transportation, restaurants, hospitals in which you can render essential war service.

Hitler will not come to our shores if we build the ships which can transport our soldiers and our war material overseas. We are turning the armies, we are building the airplanes, tanks, guns, and trucks, to do the job that must be done. But they will be of little use if we do not build the ships that can transport them to the battle zones.

Many of you are already in war jobs and are rendering essential service to our common country in the hour of need. We do not ask that you give up one essential job to take another. "We do appeal to you, however, to take a job in which you can aid the war program. Those of you who are not engaged in war work or essential civilian employment, we do urge you to take the training which will equip you for such jobs NOW without delay.

Women have responded nobly to the call to war work throughout the Nation. Many are employed in the shipyards in Mobile now. Many are at Brookley Field. Still others are in plants which are producing the war supplies essential to victory. Women who have never worked before are employed in plants and other necessary business establishments. Women have proved their efficiency in war work. Throughout our country they are doing work which many believed could be done only by men.

In many war plants women make up more than 30 per cent of the workers. In some war plants they constitute 70 per cent of the employment list. In one war plant every employee is a woman. In another plant where before the war the hiring policy was "No Women," women are in 35 per cent of the jobs and are being hired as fast as they can be found. In the Norfolk navy yards 500 women are employed as mechanics. They operate lathes, serve as drill press operators and shapers, assemble engines, repair radios, generators and electric starters, and do repair work. The United States Employment Service, after long study, has reported that, "It can hardly be said that any occupation is absolutely unsuitable for the employment of women. Women have shown that they can do or learn to do almost any kind of work."

Four million women are now employed in America's war industries. Fifteen million women are employed in other jobs which

have released men for the armed services and other essential war work. But this is not enough. Six million additional women must go into jobs essential to maximum war production. Every housewife should ask herself and answer this question: "Can I be of greater service in my home or in a war plant?" If she finds that her children can be cared for in a nursery or by a home nurse, relative or friend, then she should take the training which will equip her for a job in a war plant or an essential civilian industry.

A recent survey of Mobile shows that approximately 6,400 women are unemployed and available for war work. This does not include women who have come into Mobile with their husbands in recent months. Many of them might serve. It does not include women whose daily presence is required in their homes.

Every woman in Mobile who is willing to take an essential job can get the training and can be referred to a job as soon as she completes a short training course. There are idle training machines in Mobile. One is waiting for you. You may get training in welding, machine shops, drafting and tracing, sheet metal, and ship electricity. Every business in Mobile has a training program, either in its plant or in a training course elsewhere. You may select your course. Supervisors will recommend courses which you can readily master and which will lead to war jobs without delay. The United States Employment Service, 107 Government Street, will be glad to tell you about them.

If you can't take a permanent job you are needed for essential volunteer service by the Mobile Council of Defense. You can fill many jobs in the civilian defense program. Every woman in Mobile can render an essential service as a worker in a war plant, in an essential civilian industry or in the civilian service program of the Council of Defense.

Every woman has an opportunity to register for an essential job or for a training course. Registration booths will be opened by the United States Employment Service at public schools and many other places in Mobile at 9 a.m. Monday, February 22. They will be open from 9 a.m. to 8 p.m. each day through Saturday, February 27. Women volunteers, who have been trained to fill out the registration cards used by the United States Employment Service, will be in charge of the booths.

Every woman in Mobile who can take an essential job or training for a job is urged at this time of national crisis as a good American to register with the United States Employment Service during this Women's Registration Week. Remember: Every woman who takes a job hastens the day of victory for American arms—AND PEACE.

Help bring them back alive!

WAR MANPOWER COMMISSION
United States Employment Service

THIS PAGE IS SPONSORED BY THESE PATRIOTIC MOBILE BUSINESSES!

Alabama Stationery Co.
Battle House
B. F. Goodrich Silvertown Stores
Bond's Jewelry
C. J. Gayfer & Co.
Coca-Cola Bottling Co.
Constantine's
Damrich Shoe Store
Delchamps Stores
DeVan Motor Co.
Ferd Zundel, Jeweler
Firestone Stores
Frank H. Stoll
Franklin's
Goldstein's
Greater Zoghby Store
Greer's Stores
Gulf Coast Motor Co.
Haas-Davis Packing Co.
Hammel's
Hamrich Motor Co.
Hat Box
Kohn Jewelry Co.
Leader Department Store

McGowin-Lyons Hdwe. & Supply Co.
McPhillips Mfg. Co.
Marshall's Electrik Maid Bake Shops
Mobile Light & Railroad Company
Motor Parts & Supply Co.
M. P. Lindsey Lumber Co.
New Dixie Cafe
Palace Laundry & Dry Cleaners
Palliser 7-up Bottling Co.
People's Credit Clothiers
Pittsburgh Plate Glass Co.
Prichard Furniture Co.
Reiss Bros.
Ripps Department Store
Roxy Theater
Sam Joy Laundry
Sears, Roebuck & Co.
S. H. Kress & Co.
Sokol's
Weatherby Furniture Co.
Yon & Boylan Motor Co.

In recruiting women for war industries in 1943, the War Manpower Commission suggested in this advertisement that non-employed women were shirkers: "There are idle machines in war plants which you can operate. . . . Practically all available man-power has been exhausted, so the solving of the problem rests with the women." (*Mobile Press Register*, February 21, 1943; courtesy of University of South Alabama Library) change from a desk job to the assembly line? Am I too old for factory work?"[14]

The War Manpower Commission encouraged women with the words, "We do not believe that you Women of Mobile will shirk your responsibility . . . we believe you will rally to the call now." Women were cautioned, however, not to give up one essential job for another. But if their job was not essential, they were to enroll in one of the training programs for war work. The WMC observed that women had responded well in other areas and had proven to be efficient in war work: "Today women are doing work which many believed could be done only by men."[15]

The USES optimistically estimated that sixty-four hundred women were not employed, were able to work, and should register. This estimate turned out to be totally unrealistic. Crowds flocked to obtain ration books, but few women signed up for defense jobs. Only fifteen hundred to two thousand women registered, and a thousand of these did not want full-time work or to take training courses. One worker who was registering women observed, "It looks as though the women are waiting to be drafted."[16] Morley tied to put the best possible face on the situation by suggesting that other women would register later and claiming that the USES office was receiving calls daily.

Actually Morley's experience was not unique. Throughout the war, fewer women responded to the call to work in defense plants than government officials and others expected. Women's decisions to work depended on a wide variety of factors, the least of which probably were government recruitment drives. Women refused to be manipulated in and out of the labor force by government agencies. The WMC set unrealistic goals and then blamed women for being slackers when they did not respond to recruitment drives as anticipated. An editorial in the *Mobile Register* entitled "Behind the Women's Reluctance" concluded that the real reason women did not volunteer was that they did not fully understand the manpower shortage. The writer implied that if they did, they would volunteer; he concluded that "American women are not slackers."[17]

The recruiting themes used during both of these major drives were similar to those advanced by the War Manpower Commission. The WMC was in an ambivalent position regarding the recruiting of women. It wanted and needed their labor yet at the same time wanted to maintain the traditional female role at home. Thus women were encouraged to step out of the usual role for the duration in the name of patriotism and the family. Wartime employment, then, marked only a temporary retreat from the prevailing notions of women's abilities and proper roles. Even though the image of the American woman changed from that of wife, mother, and home-maker to that of war worker, these changes were superficial. Lelia J. Rupp has said, "They were meant by the government and under-stood by the public, to be temporary. . . . Rosie was still primarily a wife and mother, and her factory job could be viewed as an exten-sion of these duties."[18]

The WMC revealed its ambivalent position by maintaining its belief that a woman's first duty was to her children, despite the need for female labor. The commission made it clear that the situation was not severe enough that women with young children to care for at home should undertake regular full-time war jobs outside the home. Such women were to be recruited only as a last resort and only if adequate care was provided for their children. Despite this policy statement, women with young children were recruited in areas of labor shortages and adequate child care was not always provided. Mobile recruiters took any woman who sought employ-ment and were only marginally concerned with providing child care.

All of the recruitment drives in Alabama were aimed at the un-employed housewife, not at women who had had working experi-ence. The government ignored women's history of work in factories since the beginning of industrialization. Presumably the 24 percent of the prewar Alabama labor force that was female did not have to be encouraged to seek employment. Housewives always made up a minority of women recruited for war work; for example, in Mobile only 23 percent of the employed women had been engaged in house-work before the war. None of the campaigns was aimed at black women, even though they outnumbered white women in the work

force by two to one. The image of the white middle-class housewife
turned factory worker was the dominant wartime public theme.[19]

Indeed, wartime jobs were compared to housework in an attempt
to convince women that they could do such work. Munition making
was compared to running a sewing machine or a vacuum cleaner.
The Mobile Air Service Command tried to recruit women to repair
airplane instruments with the message: "If you can operate a sewing
machine, open a can of tomatoes, take a vacuum cleaner half apart
or make emergency repairs on the refrigerator, you can help defeat
the Axis."[20] This approach may have been intended to assure women
that they could do war work, but it also reinforced the idea that
women's talents lay in homemaking and that they did not intend to
be a permanent part of the work force.

Not only was war work compared to housework, but it was sometimes made to appear almost like a picnic. One of the first welders
in the shipyards was quoted as saying: "Welding is fun, and really
an art." Other women were described as happy in their jobs. While
wearing helmets, they always had a happy smile and a merry word
for their coworkers.[21] The purpose of this approach was to convince
women that war work was not as difficult as they might think.

Great care was taken to preserve the traditional image of femininity for women war workers. The message was conveyed that women
might be doing men's jobs, they might even dress like men, but
underneath they were still women. Even though women worked as
welders in the Mobile shipyards wearing heavy clothing and helmets,
"here and there something feminine appears. On a straw hat there's
a gay flowered ribbon and sticking out from under a coverall are red
leather oxfords." Pictures of women welders with their helmets
pushed back while they applied lipstick assured readers that these
workers were still feminine.[22]

Women war workers were portrayed as attractive wives and mothers who were sacrificing home life for patriotism. Recruitment propaganda appealed to altruism and affection rather than to base
motives of high pay. The public was constantly and incorrectly told
that women did not have to work for a living. The implication was that

they did not take war jobs because they needed money but because "women must step in to take the place of men in vital war industries." The women who worked at the Huntsville Arsenal were said to believe that "the money side of the job . . . [was] considered secondary."[23] Such attitudes allowed women to be recruited to do men's work without making any permanent change in "women's place."

The major recruiting theme was an appeal to patriotism. Women war workers were urged to fulfill their duty as citizens to help hasten victory. The theme of the February 1943 Mobile campaign was "Every Woman Who Takes a Job Hastens the Day of Victory for American Arms and Peace." The national campaign of the WMC shortened this theme the next month to "The More Women at Work, the Sooner We'll Win."[24] Both slogans asked women to do their part in a positive way. Women could save lives by taking jobs and thus help win the war sooner.

This patriotic appeal could also be used in a negative way by containing a threat. The regional informational representative of the WMC said, "If we don't get these women to work, we won't be able to equip our soldiers and . . . it will prolong the war indefinitely. The women recruiting plan is necessary in this district particularly because we are not winning the battle of the Atlantic and we need the ships that are being built here. . . . The War Manpower Commission wants to ask women if they're good Americans and if they will go to work."[25] This approach contains the obvious implication that if women did not work they were not patriotic citizens. Idle women were viewed as a threat to the armed forces and the nation.

These recruitment drives were all aimed at young, white, middle-class housewives who supposedly did not need to work but who would do so out of patriotic motives. The government viewed married women without children under the age of ten as the best source of war workers. Not only were these women available, but it was further assumed that they would leave their work at the end of the war and return to homemaking, thus leaving jobs for returning veterans. This image reflected incorrect assumptions at the highest levels of government and industry about women workers.[26]

The long-standing myths about the role of wage labor in women's lives were that married women sought employment only to enable their families to buy "extras" and that single women worked only until they married and then dropped out. Wage labor was merely an adjunct to women's "real" role, which was full-time homemaking and childrearing. Yet the women who entered war production were working-class wives, widows, divorcees, students, and black women who needed the money to achieve a decent standard of living. The majority of these women had had prewar experience in the labor force. They worked during the war because they had to support themselves or someone else; they worked for the same reasons men did—because they needed the income. In Mobile, for example, 55 percent of the women who joined the work force had worked before the war and 82 percent had to support themselves and others.[27] The wartime demands may have added some new motivations to women's economic decisions, but material considerations always remained paramount.

The third and last recruitment drive conducted by the WMC in Mobile was held in April 1944 and corresponded roughly to the final national drive, although it was aimed at both women and men. During March, the USES announced that Alabama was in immediate and pressing need for 17,136 additional war workers, approximately 25 percent of them in the Mobile area. The campaign was initiated in April, when a door-to-door search was conducted to locate workers. Women and men who were not employed or not engaged in essential work were encouraged to take defense jobs. Defense workers were pictured as leaders of style in the 1944 Easter Parade wearing their welding clothes and helmets. By June 1944, women were being urged to "Work for—Not Wait for—Victory."[28]

Concurrent with the drives to recruit war workers was the establishment of a variety of training programs, which by the fall of 1942 were actively seeking women. The government first made use of the National Youth Administration (NYA), a New Deal agency, to offer programs in Mobile, Birmingham, Tuscaloosa, Auburn, and Normal. The NYA program in Mobile accepted only men and women with previous training and placed them directly in industries as soon as possible. Potential war workers went to Mobile, not only from Alabama but also from Georgia, Florida, Mississippi, and Arkansas. The Mobile induction center offered courses in welding, sheet metal work, machine shop operation, and machine fitting. Headlines in the *Birmingham News* read, "Girls . . . are finding an answer to the question, 'How can I help fight the war?' " These "girls" were offered an opportunity to learn to use machines once operated only by men. The Birmingham NYA accepted unemployed women from the ages of seventeen to twenty-five for training in sheet metal work, pattern making, and power sewing. Some three hundred women in Birmingham enrolled in this program, which was designed to run two to three months.[29]

The federal government established two new programs to train war workers, both of which offered courses in Alabama. The first, Vocational Training for War Production Workers (VTWPW), established vocational training classes for women in Mobile in September 1942. Women could not be admitted to this program until a need for their labor existed, but by late 1942 the labor shortage was sufficiently severe to warrant their admission. Headlines announced "Facilities Prepare to Train Fairer Sex," as courses in welding, drafting, pipefitting, pipe covering, plumbing, carpentry, and electrical work were opened to women. Three hundred women began training as electric-arc welders, burners, and machinists, but the percentage of women in these classes remained small.[30]

In another federally sponsored program—Engineering, Science, and Management War Training (ESMWT)—the major universities of the state, the University of Alabama, Alabama Polytechnic Institute (Auburn University), Howard College (Samford University), and Birmingham-Southern College, offered a large number of college-level courses free of charge. No black colleges in Alabama received ESMWT funds because none offered a four-year course leading to a professional degree in engineering, chemistry, physics, or production supervision. These courses were also open to women, and a few even aimed their advertisements directly at them. The University

of Alabama specifically sought women for a shipdrafting course in
November 1942, and twelve women enrolled. Howard College offered a popular course for women in engineering drawing followed
by a course in tool engineering, structural engineering, electrical
engineering, or engineering mathematics. In December 1942, 30
percent of the registrants in Alabama were women. No figures are
available on how many women finished the courses and obtained
war production jobs.[31] After mid-1943, few women or men sought
training because the supply of labor was so short that a worker could
obtain a job without training. There was little incentive to forego
pay for a training period when a high-paying job was available. After
this time virtually all workers received on-the-job training.[32]

Black women had difficulty obtaining training despite President
Franklin D. Roosevelt's creation of the Fair Employment Practices
Committee (FEPC) to ban racial discrimination in war industries.
Roosevelt had acted only after black labor leader A. Philip Randolph
had threatened a massive march on Washington in 1941. The U.S.
Employment Service in Alabama issued a policy statement that read:
"Every person, regardless of sex or race, not now in a war job or
engaged in farming should register with the nearest office of the
Employment Service."[33] When black women tried to register for
training, however, they were turned away.

Two black women, Margaret Davis Frazier and Zemma D. Camphor, were refused admission to a training program at Brookley Field
in 1943. Both had passed the Mechanic Learner Test but were told
that Brookley did not have training classes for blacks. The women
filed complaints with the FEPC, and eventually a training school for
blacks was established. Black women at Bechtel-McCone-Parsons
Corporation were not so fortunate. The plant reluctantly accepted
black women for training but then refused to give them jobs. Company officials counseled them to "sit tight and be satisfied that they
were collecting wages as trainees." Emory O. Jackson, editor of the
Birmingham World, pointed out that such an attitude flouted established federal policy and depressed the morale of blacks in the area.[34]

As a result of such practices, most black women became discouraged and ceased seeking training.

By 1943, as the draft began to deplete the male labor supply, the government turned to female workers for the defense industries in order to maintain production. The recruitment drives were aimed to persuade the white middle-class housewife to become a war worker by stressing the similarity between housework and industrial work. Alabama women heeded the nation's call and entered the work force in record numbers. They responded to the recruitment drives, not from patriotic motives of self-sacrifice but because they had an opportunity to earn a real wage. I will now consider where women worked, what jobs they performed, under what conditions they worked, and why they entered the work force.

CHAPTER 3

Women as

Defense Workers

The largest number of women who were employed in defense industries during the war found work in Mobile, where they worked either at Brookley Field repairing and servicing airplanes or at the shipyards building liberty ships, tankers, and minesweepers. The second greatest number worked in Birmingham at numerous jobs, the most important of which was the modification of airplanes. Third in importance was employment at the ordnance works and arsenals in Huntsville and Childersburg. Finally, substantial numbers of women continued to be employed in textile mills that had war contracts. How many women were actually employed? What exactly did they do? How were they received by their male coworkers? What was the experience of black women? How were women perceived by the public? And finally, why did these women work? These are the questions to answer if we are to understand the new role of women as defense workers.

The Mobile Air Service Command at Brookley Field was by far the largest employer of women in the state. At its height in March 1944 MoASC employed approximately seventy-five hundred women.[1] Brookley Field, where the command was located, was officially established in October 1939 by the army air force, but little construction was undertaken until early 1940. After the war began, the air force recognized the need for a service command to supply

Women work alongside men to repair instruments at Mobile's Brookley
Field during the war. (Courtesy of University of South Alabama Photographic
Archives)

and maintain the large numbers of planes that would be required.
As a result, the Air Service Command was created in October of
1941 as a separate branch of the army air force. By late 1942 the
status of the command was changed from a military organization to
an industrial one whose duties were to furnish supplies, provide
repairs, and overhaul and rebuild army air force airplanes throughout
the world. The Mobile Air Service Command was one of nineteen
depots in the United States and overseas.[2]

MoASC experienced much difficulty in securing an adequate number of civilian employees in labor-short Mobile. Its attempts to
recruit workers in nearby states were limited by the lack of housing
in the area. Hence the command turned to the local population,
following the advice of the regional director of the WMC, who said
that winning the war required employing people who were not
normally employed such as handicapped persons, older people, and

THE WORKING DAUGHTERS OF BROOKLEY FIELD

MoASC TERMED
"NO-MAN'S-LAND"
BROOKLEY WOMEN DESERVE PRAISE AND
COMMENDATION FOR THEIR CON-
TRIBUTION TO WAR EFFORT

by Muriel C. Fernandez

The Mobile Air Service Command
is rapidly approaching the stage
where it could almost be termed a
"No-Man's Land." It is estimated
at this time that approximately
50% of the civilians now employed
at Brookley Field are women, and
indications are that by January,
1944, they will comprise at least
75% of our workers.

One can stroll through any department on the Post, and not
fail to be impressed by the fact
that tasks heretofore performed
exclusively by men are now being
efficiently done by members of
the "weaker sex." Housewives,
schoolgirls, social butterflies,
waitresses, store clerks - these

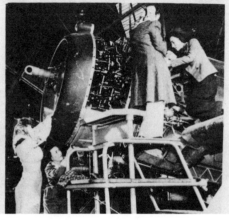

Women mechanics work on the engine of an A-24 aircraft in Brookley Field
repair hangar, July 5, 1943. (*A la Moad,* courtesy of Municipal Archives,
City of Mobile)

married women. MoASC broke new ground by being one of the first
to employ large numbers of women and the first to train and employ
handicapped people on a large scale. By 1943 Brookley employed
seventeen thousand people, almost half of whom were women and
eight hundred of whom were physically handicapped.[3] MoASC also
employed some black women after complaints had been lodged with
the Fair Employment Practices Committee.

Women were employed in all departments and divisions of the
Mobile Air Service Command, but the most unusual jobs they held
involved the repair and maintenance of airplanes. Women inspected
the engines, repaired the fuselages, welded parts together, riveted
sheet metal, and prepared the engines for combat use. The Engineering Department created a "crack girl crew" of five to work
together to inspect and repair the planes. This checking required
infinite attention to detail, at which women were thought to excel.
Women also repaired camera and navigation instruments, electrical
instruments, general instruments, and gyro instruments. They were

regarded as being more capable than men for such work because they were better at handling the intricate parts.[4] It was widely believed that women liked these boring and repetitive tasks that would drive men crazy.

Large numbers of women were employed in the Supply Division to do clerical jobs such as handling property accounts, reports, contracts, files, teletype, and correspondence. But they also worked in the warehouse section, where they handled the vast quantities of material that constituted air corps inventories. They worked in the receiving, storage, packing, shipping, and stenciling departments, filling positions that were normally held by men. The civilian supply inspector said, "They are proving highly satisfactory in their work. . . . I am sure this step will help solve the acute shortage of inspectors we have . . . experienced." These "working daughters of Brookley Field" were slowly "taking over" the depot supply. According to the MoASC newsletter, the fair sex was not afraid to do men's jobs. Women who might have been referred to as "housewives, school girls, social butterflies, waitresses, store clerks" were now an integral part of one of the country's largest and most important depots.[5]

The Mobile Air Service Command made use of women as drivers for the numerous government staff cars. Each woman had to take a course in motor mechanics and pass a difficult driving test before being considered a qualified driver. Women were expected to be able to change flat tires and make minor adjustments to motors. These feminine drivers released men for more important jobs. They were described as giving a "new twist to the 'Woman I saw you out with last night' gag." One female driver stated that the wives of the officers they drove need "have no cause for alarm. Many of us are wives too, and we are all interested in the progress of the war effort." One MoASC newsletter even showed a picture of a woman opening the automobile door for a male officer.[6]

The first women guards at an army post in the United States served at Brookley Field beginning in September of 1942. They received training in fire prevention, first aid, sabotage and espionage prevention, traffic control, and self-protection. Most of them had had two

years of college. On duty they wore navy blue uniforms, Sam Browne
belts, overseas caps, and low-heeled shoes. The lieutenant in charge
of the civilian guards said: "These girls don't know it yet, but they'll
have to stand out in the rain and take it on the chin just like all the
other guards. They'll have to work shifts . . . and will hand in reports
in the same manner as men guards do now. The only distinction will
be that women will be unarmed."[7]

The Mobile Air Service Command also pioneered in the employment of the handicapped. As early as July 1942, through an agreement with the Civil Service and Vocational Rehabilitation
Department, forty to fifty handicapped people were employed. By
October the number had increased to five hundred, and in February
1943, approximately eight hundred were employed. The number
eventually reached fourteen hundred by March 1944. Many of these
were women. A survey was conducted to determine what work they
could perform. Blind people were adept at cleaning spark plugs;
others who were blind, such as Ruth Cunningham and Margherita
Koppersmith, packed bolts by their weight. Eileen Sutton, who had
been blind for thirty-five years, worked as a typist. A deaf woman,
Emily T. Rugsby, did good work repairing gyro instruments. Absenteeism among these people was virtually unknown.[8]

Another woman who might not have gained employment under
peacetime conditions was tiny Ruby C. Tipton, who was only four
feet two inches tall and weighed 62 pounds. She found her small
size to be an advantage in her work in the electrical department.
Another worker in the same department was Martha Buck, who was
five feet eight inches tall and weighed 280 pounds. These two women
were pictured in the newsletter with the caption, "Large and Small
Work Side by Side at MoASC." Even age was not a barrier to
employment, as Kate V. Lyons learned. She celebrated her sixty-
eighth birthday on her job sewing engine and cockpit covers.[9]

Brookley Field also employed black women, but only after
the FEPC forced it to establish a training program. Even then
black women worked primarily in low-paying and low-skilled jobs.
Margaret Davis Frazier and Zemma D. Camphor, who gained the

right to attend a training program, were employed as a maid and a laborer. Camphor soon discovered that she was doing the work of a mechanic helper without being paid for it. One black woman commented that she would have liked to work at Brookley but did not because of indignities and humiliations suffered at the hands of white coworkers. She said, "All these things hurt." Another black woman was refused employment at Brookley but later obtained a job in the kitchen of the Battle House Hotel.[10] MoASC newsletters were full of information on white women but never contained items about black women, despite the presence of black employees.

In addition to being the first depot to employ large numbers of women, MoASC also was one of the first to receive a contingent of the Women's Army Corps. In February 1944 the first enlisted WACs arrived, "trim and spruce, and burdened with barracks bags." For the next two years other khaki-clad women joined the original group until at its height the squadron numbered more than two hundred. The novelty of seeing women soldiers took time to wear off, but soon they were as accepted as the giant superfortresses that took off from the runways. When the units were deactivated in December 1945, the editor of the newspaper wrote: "They have done their jobs well and have earned fine commendations from their superiors. Brookley Field won't seem quite the same without them but we know they're happy to be going home again and so we say—Goodbye Ladies— and Good Luck."[11]

Brookley Field may have employed the largest number of women, but those women who received the most publicity worked as welders, burners, and electricians in the shipyards. In the course of the war the percentage of women employed in the shipyards varied from 9 to 11; in absolute numbers this meant from twenty-eight hundred to thirty-five hundred. Some were welders, but almost half were engaged in more traditional office work.[12]

Shipbuilding had always been a male bastion. Before the war women were not employed in the shipyards even in the offices. Hence women welders were nearly as much of a novelty as women soldiers. Since welding was viewed as an unusual and temporary

Ida M. Broadway was one of the first women employed as a welder at
ADDSCO in Mobile. She worked continuously until the war ended in 1945.
(Courtesy of ADDSCO Collection, University of South Alabama Photo-
graphic Archives)

job, the public tended to trivialize the role of women welders by
referring to them as "lady welders" or "welderettes." Welding was
hard, uncomfortable work that attracted few women. Welders had
to work in the hot Alabama sun; they had to wear long sleeves to
protect their arms from burns. They also wore welding helmets and
kneeled on hard metals while they welded, all the while enduring
the thunderous noise of the shipyard. The management of the shipyards was reluctant to employ women. Both the WMC and the USES
put pressure on the shipyards to employ them because by 1943 to
do so was official U.S. policy. All during the war the shipyards
employed women only as a last resort when the supply of available
men had been exhausted.[13]

The Alabama Dry Docks and Shipbuilding Company began hiring

women as early as July 1942. One of the first to be employed was Ida M. Broadway, who worked continuously through the war. Broadway worked out on the platens at the port side of Ways 11, where she wove molten metal into the seams of plates. She saw a similarity between her work in the shipyard and her previous job as a seamstress: "These plates and stiffeners are cut by patterns to proper length, they are fitted and tacked together—just like basting a skirt or dress, and then we weld the seams. The only difference is the material is hard and the stitches are hot." At the war's end she had worked longer for the company than any other woman.[14]

ADDSCO established "all-girl" crews to work together. Welding crews on Ways 7 made up entirely of women were still working together at the war's end. The crew consisted of fourteen members under a male supervisor who praised the women as having done a "swell job." Another all-women production group assembled the electrical shipboard panel sections. At one time these eight women set a record in assembling the main shaft in five hours when it was needed in a hurry. They were described by their foreman as "doing a fine job."[15] The management probably believed that women would be more easily accepted by and would work better with other women; these particular all-women crews were the exception, however, because most women worked in mixed crews.

Some women attained leadership positions, but they were few in number. In July 1944 several women were advanced to the position of "leaderwoman." Mrs. R. B. Harleson was promoted to leaderwoman in the fabrication shop layout department. Harleson, who had worked as a cashier in a Mobile store before the war, had studied mechanical drawing in high school and college. She supervised a crew of fourteen layout workers, some of whom were men. Some thirteen other women were also promoted to leadership positions at the same time.[16] These promotions received much publicity because the women were a distinct minority.

Other women worked as machinists, drill press operators, burners, pipe threaders, boilermakers, electrical maintenance workers, and time checkers. Still others held more traditional jobs in the

Top: This woman, like virtually all women employed at Mobile's ADDSCO shipyards during the war, worked for a male supervisor. *Above:* Among the wartime jobs assigned to women at ADDSCO was engine repair. (Both photos courtesy of ADDSCO Collection, University of South Alabama Photographic Archives)

offices of the companies as clerks, secretaries, telephone operators, nurses, mail carriers, and time keepers. Women also worked as uniformed guards at the shipyards. They were used in this capacity because of the shortage of men but also because women worked in the plants. They served in clerical roles, as escorts, and as guards throughout the yard, mainly at points where women worked. The presence of women compelled the company to reverse an age-old custom and allow women aboard ships for the first time. The question of whether the women would be armed was not immediately determined. The public found it difficult to take women guards seriously, as shown by the suggestion of one observer that the women could be armed with hatpins, rubber blackjacks, or the more familiar rolling pin. [17]

Black women were employed by ADDSCO as ship-sweepers and cleaners, cleaning out the bottoms of ships, loading boxcars, picking up scrap iron in the yard, and other odd jobs. Black women were never given higher-paying jobs as welders or burners. Margaret Bernard said, "They wont let the colored women Weld or Burn. I would like to go to Tuskegee to learn Welding and Burning, but I know if I did, I would have to go up North in order to Weld or Burn." Another black woman asked, "Are they ever going to allow colored women to get any jobs in Alabama Drydocks where they can get more than 63 cents an hour? I worked at this place 18 months with no raise, no promotion." The experience of these black women was similar to that of blacks in other shipyards, where they did the dirtiest jobs for the lowest wages. [18]

In Birmingham the largest employer of women was the newly established Bechtel-McCone-Parsons airplane modification plant. In February 1942, the Birmingham Chamber of Commerce conducted a survey of women asking if they would work in a defense plant if one were located in Birmingham. More than eight thousand women responded that they would be interested in such employment. The large supply of female labor was evidently one factor influencing the company's decision to select Birmingham over Atlanta or New Orleans because it intended to hire twelve to fifteen thousand work-

In this series of artificially posed promotional photographs, women were spotlighted in two spheres of activity formerly restricted to men: shipyard work and military service. The two new roles were juxtaposed in these scenes without regard for realism; ordinarily, WACS would have had no assignments requiring them to stand about observing women welders at work. (Courtesy of ADDSCO Collection, University of South Alabama Photographic Archives)

ers. The Bechtel-McCone-Parsons plant began training both men
and women in early February 1943 while the plant was still being
constructed. The goal was to have twenty-five hundred workers
trained by March 15. The airplane plant used the vocational facilities
of the local high schools as well as those of the University of Alabama
and Alabama Polytechnic Institute. The preemployment training
lasted three weeks, and men and women with previous experience
received fifty cents per hour. Minimum age for women was sixteen;
for men it was eighteen.[19]

By March of 1943 Bechtel-McCone-Parsons's work force was 43.8
percent female; however, in July the percentage dropped to 41.6
and in September to 29 percent. During July and August 1943 the
company experienced a severe crisis that threatened its future. Initially it overestimated the number of employees it would need and
hired more people than were necessary. Then, during the summer,
the planes that were scheduled to be modified failed to arrive on
time, and the corporation was forced to lay off nearly twenty-three
hundred workers between July and September 1943. The majority
of these were women.[20] In addition to being overstaffed, the plant
was investigated by the War Department, the Truman War Defense
Committee, and the House Military Affairs Committee. Bechtel-
McCone-Parsons was charged with defrauding the government of
$1 million in unnecessary labor, materials, and training programs.

Eventually the company was cleared of all the charges. It rehired
old workers, began new training programs, and met the production
schedules. The company expanded production and by 1944 it employed nearly ten thousand workers, two thousand more than earlier;
of these 37 percent were women. These figures remained fairly
constant until the end of the war. The corporation relied heavily on
untrained personnel from the local area; 86 percent of employees
had no previous training, and only 10 percent came from other
industries. The other 80 percent were drawn from nonessential
industries and included clerks, students, barbers, and previously
unemployed housewives.[21]

Despite the reliance on local untrained workers, few black women

were employed by Bechtel-McCone-Parsons. The Birmingham
USES refused to refer black women to the plant for jobs. Martha
Riley's experience was typical. She filled out an application for employment and was told "they would call me when they get a open
for me and they never do and I goes Back down there every week
and they tell me the same thing over and over." Another black
woman, Mary B. Summers, wrote, "I have complied with all rules
such as filling Blanks is concerned . . . and they tell us to go to the
state employment office and get said Blanks and bring them to the
said place and we do this and you [President Roosevelt] tell us to
work or fight and we want to work and there is plenty to do and yet
we colored peoples some of us cant get jobs and these plants and
places say we need you and yet they still hire all white ladies and no
colored only a few can get jobs." Despite the policies of the FEPC,
the Birmingham USES refused to cooperate in reporting and seeking
to change discriminatory practices. Bechtel-McCone-Parsons refused to employ black women in the modification plant and gave
them work only as maids. Denying blacks the opportunity to work
in skilled war jobs increased the racial tension in Birmingham, according to Emory O. Jackson, editor of the black newspaper, *Birmingham World.*[22]

Women were also employed in the ordnance plants in the state.
The Alabama Ordnance Works, constructed by the DuPont Corporation and located at Childersburg, manufactured smokeless powder,
TNT, and Tetryl. The Brecon Loading Company bagged the black
powder and smokeless powder for artillery shells. Located near
Talladega, this company was, of the two, the larger employer of
women. These two plants together overwhelmed the small towns of
Talladega, Childersburg, and Sylacauga with more than fourteen
thousand employees by March 1943. The number dropped to around
seven thousand by September of that year, but it increased to ten
thousand by September 1944. The Brecon Company employed almost 50 percent women in March 1943; the proportion fell to a low
of 28 percent in September 1943 but rose again to 45.7 percent in
September of the following year.

Female employment in the Alabama Ordnance Works was never expected to be large. In March it was only 7 percent, but by September 1944 it had gradually increased to 17 percent. Women were not viewed as capable of performing the higher-paying work in the ordnance works, but the work in the Brecon plant of weighing the powder, pouring it into a bag, and sewing it shut was considered more appropriate to females. The wages paid by both companies reflected the skill and danger involved in the operations. The Alabama Ordnance plant paid skilled labor $300 per month, semi-skilled $225, and unskilled $140, whereas the Brecon Company paid only $110 to $115 per month. Brecon had difficulty keeping employees because of the low wages. To maintain its work force, it had to relax hiring practices to permit the employment of married women.[23]

Despite the need for workers, the Brecon plant was not willing to employ black women until pressured to do so by the FEPC. Hearings conducted in Birmingham by the FEPC in June 1943 resulted in the Brecon Company employing a few token black women. This policy did not last long; by 1944 the company together with the Talladega USES office was once again refusing to employ blacks. USES officials divided their applications into white and colored sections with "W" and "C" marked on the applications, a practice that was in violation of FEPC rulings. After a year-long investigation, the office abandoned the policy, but the Brecon Company continued its discriminatory policy. A black woman, Evelyn Keith, applied for work on four different occasions. She observed that the plant "takes over 40 or 50 white girls Every Week But us colored one they say to us we not taken on Any Negro girls now that not fair The war is not Being fought By the White men alone The niger is They call us is sure in it as well. it sure is Bad here how they treat us colored peoples."[24]

In Huntsville both the Redstone Arsenal and the Huntsville Arsenal employed substantial numbers of women. Redstone manufactured grenades, bombs, and shells, and the Huntsville Arsenal, operated by the Chemical Warfare Service, manufactured toxic gas. The total employment of both operations averaged between ninety-five hundred and ten thousand people; female employment ran

Women working at Redstone Arsenal at Huntsville during the war. (Courtesy of Redstone Arsenal)

around 30 to 35 percent. These women were described as handling the tough tasks of the "stronger sex." In the Huntsville Arsenal a successful all-"girl" line was established in the fill and press building. The workers were described as "modern Amazons" from Madison County who broke all records. Several of them received men's wages, although their high pay was viewed by the public as secondary to their personal stake in winning the war.[25]

Southern textile plants, which had depended heavily upon female labor before the war, continued to employ record numbers of women. Virtually all textile mills had war contracts to manufacture a wide variety of items, such as Arctic helmets, uniform twills, pistol belts, first aid pouches, bandoleers, helmet chin straps, surgical elastic, machine gun belts, parachute harnesses, target tow line, rope, tents, and barracks bags. Textile mills employed approximately 45 percent women in Sylacauga and Anniston, 50 percent in Gadsden, and 64 percent in Decatur.[26]

Alabama women worked not only in defense plants but also in a wide variety of professional and service jobs that did not usually employ women. As early as 1941, county health departments appointed women physicians as health officers, which was the first time female doctors had held such responsibility. In 1943 the Tutwiler Prison for women appointed the first female superintendent; the appointment of a woman warden had been a long-time goal of the Committee on Pardons and Parole. Other women had jobs as automobile mechanics, stock board markers, pharmacists, school bus drivers, police complaint clerks, and clerks in the state legislature.[27]

Alabama black women did have one unique opportunity for skilled employment. They could work at the Tuskegee Army Flying School, the only training school for black pilots in the nation. The training program was based at the Tuskegee Institute, which had been founded by Booker T. Washington in 1881. Women worked in the ground crews, as air craft dispatchers and electricians, in the repair and maintenance division, and as office workers. At Tuskegee black women had an unusual opportunity to serve in skilled wartime jobs to "Keep 'em Flying" at an army airfield. One can only estimate how many women found employment there, but the number must have been small because black men hired black women as reluctantly as white men employed white women. The majority of the employees at the airfield were doubtless male. The black newspaper, the *Birmingham World,* said that the efficiency with which the weaker sex found employment in war industries and as army personnel was a "convincing revelation of their unusual aptness and adaptability. The 'red bandana' has been discarded for earphones and the kitchen apron packed away for leather and rubber aprons for the duration."[28]

Another opportunity for black women at Tuskegee was in nurses' training. In 1940 the federal government selected John Anderson Memorial Hospital in Tuskegee as a training center for the U.S. Cadet Nurse Corps. Black women came from all over the Southeast to enroll in the nine-month training program. Because of the serious shortage of nurses, local black women also had access to training programs in city hospitals. The number of black nurses increased not only in Alabama but nationwide.[29] Nursing was, of course, a

Did someone say this is a man's war ?

What about the women here on the home front? They're
doing men's jobs in hundreds of great war plants, working
long hours in stores and offices, driving buses and
running street cars, giving their time and toil to many
war-vital purposes. . . . *They are saving men's
lives and speeding Victory.* This is *everybody's* war!

All those bookkeeping girls behind the scenes are
doing essential work too — and doing it well. In
many offices, National Typewriting-Bookkeeping Machines help them speed the day's work and save
precious man-hours. These machines are fast, efficient,
easy to master . . . they can be transferred from one
accounting job to another in a matter of seconds . . .
even inexperienced girls find the standard adding
machine and typewriter keyboards simple and easy
to operate.

All National products and systems play vital roles
in the war effort.

Serving the Nation by Saving Time. This is one of many mechanized
systems built by National to speed record keeping, protect money and save
vital man-hours—for business, industry, government and the public. National
Accounting-Bookkeeping Machines can be obtained through priorities.

This advertisement for National Typewriting and Bookkeeping Machines
stressed the essential war work performed by women workers on the home
front, including, of course, "those bookkeeping girls behind the scenes" who
were "serving the nation by saving time" with their "mechanized systems
built by National." (*Birmingham News*, March 7, 1944; courtesy of Alabama
Department of Archives and History)

traditional female role that did not threaten the sexual division of labor.

The majority of black women were not employed in skilled jobs but in service jobs, such as workers in laundries, cleaning women, cooks, dishwashers, bus girls, and maids. Many of these women moved from agricultural or domestic work to these jobs in service industries. Black women did not find employment in high-paying defense jobs. In Mobile, where almost a third of the employed women were black (the highest percentage in the nation), not one black woman was employed as an operative in a defense plant in 1944. In service jobs, they received the lowest wages. Women working in hotels averaged $19.45 per week, in eating and drinking places $13.95, and in laundries $16.05, whereas women working as operatives in defense plants earned $43.45 per week, and clerks in war manufacturing earned $30.30.[30]

Black women were victims of the intense racial discrimination that existed in the South during the war years. Their only recourse was to lodge a complaint with the Fair Employment Practices Committee. The records of this committee in Alabama show that a third of the complaints came from women. Even when black women could prove discrimination, the FEPC's only course was to withdraw the war contracts from the offending companies, which was unlikely when the top priority was maximum production. Even when the FEPC took action, the process was ineffective. The agency relied on individual, documented complaints rather than on employer hiring patterns as the basis for action. Often poorly educated black women had difficulty providing adequate documentation and their complaints were not investigated. By the time the FEPC had investigated, negotiated, or held hearings, much valuable time had been lost during which black women could have profited from wartime prosperity.[31]

In some cases the FEPC agreed to a settlement that only partly eliminated discrimination. An example was that of eleven black women who were fired from their jobs at the Anniston Warehouse, which was operated by the Anniston Army Depot. These women filed a complaint in December 1943 and were reinstated in March 1944 but at reduced pay. They had been receiving from $1,620 to $1,440 per year and were rehired at $1,260. They continued to feel discriminated against, especially because white workers with less experience were receiving more pay. No further action was taken before the war ended.[32] Despite the need for labor, the barriers to the employment of black women remained intact.

Because they were employed in a large number of unaccustomed roles, the public perception of women appeared to undergo a transformation. One observer believed that it would not be necessary to conscript women because they were volunteering in such large numbers: "Women who formerly thought a day's work was to get up a bridge foursome, now held down a job from 8 to 5 every day." Wide publicity was given to women who were employed in jobs formerly reserved for men. Every new breakthrough was heralded in a newspaper story. Often wives took over their husbands' jobs when they were called to the armed forces. The Business and Professional Women's Club of Birmingham was convinced that women had "become the greatest single force of labor." It celebrated the role women were playing in business and industry by sponsoring a series of conferences on such topics as "Women in Industry" and "Women and Vocational Education."[33] For the first time, their role as workers was the paramount public image of women. As Leila J. Rupp observed, "Women, for the duration, were riveting housewives in slacks, not mothers, domestic beings, or civilizers."[34] The world of the 1940s, which was built on a rigid definition of sex roles, was being challenged by this new role of women.

These changes, however, were a temporary phenomenon. The great care that was taken to preserve feminine characteristics, even though a woman might be engaged in male work, indicated the transitory nature of women's new role. The public was constantly reassured, for example, that "women welders can retain feminine beauty." The welder in question was Willie Mae Swoape, "a very pretty girl indeed," who worked as one of the welders in a crew on the North Platens in the ADDSCO yard. Other women who were

20-Year-Old Miss Willie Swoape Proves Women Welders Can Retain Feminine Beauty

She Wouldn't Trade Her Work For Job In Office; And What's More, She Buys A $25 War Bond Every Pay Day

Miss Willie Swoape, 20 years old and a very pretty girl indeed, is one of the more than 60 women welders in the crew of C. J. McClellan, foreman on the North Platens.

Miss Swoape who lives at 1569 Monterey Place, Mobile, has been a welder at Addsco for the past 11 months. During this time she has lost only one and one-half days from her job and has not been late for work a single day.

"I like to work in the open air," says Miss Swoape. "I wouldn't think about being shut up in an office."

One look at Miss Swoape's beautiful complexion will convince any one that a woman may work as a welder and still retain her feminine beauty.

Miss Swoape explained that she went to welding school for 150 hours before coming to work at Addsco. "At that time," she continued "we went to school on our own time —that is we were not paid while in training. At the present time a woman is paid a good rate while learning."

Miss Swoape is saving as well as working for victory. Every payday she buys a $25 war bond.

MISS WILLIE SWOAPE gives a welcome wave to other women to join the ranks of female welders in the yard.

"One look at Miss Swoape's beautiful complexion," according to this newspaper report, "will convince anyone that a woman may work as a welder and still retain her feminine beauty." The public seemed to require a great deal of convincing; publicity frequently stressed the femininity of women war workers. (Courtesy of City of Mobile, Museum Department)

WORKTIME AND PLAYTIME FOR BROOKLEY GIRLS

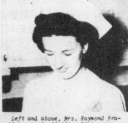

Left and above, Mrs. Raymond Bra-zil, nurse in Civilian Dispensary.

Right and above, Miss Nancy Joyce, Instrument Repair.

Left and above, Miss Thelma Harp, typist in Supply Transport.

Since any change in traditional gender roles was frightening, women workers at Brookley Field were pictured in their feminine evening dresses as well as their work clothes. (Courtesy of Municipal Archives, City of Mobile)

Mobile Draftswoman Tells How Active Hands Stay Nice

Miss Frances Bea Quigley, of 1750 H u n t e r Avenue, entered field of drafting to replace man who entered service—intends to pursue career in designing and illustrating. She says, "Even with war-work plus housework, there's no excuse for a woman to get slack about dishpan hands. I know . . . because I've learned to stop using strong washday soap for dishes. I've changed to Ivory, and now several of my friends have noticed the improvement in my hands."

You, too, can have Lovelier Hands in 12 Days

Stop using strong washday soaps for dishes . . . soaps that can leave your hands rough and red. _Put Ivory_ in your dishpan and use its _relief suds_ . . . the same pure, gentle suds doctors recommend for baby's sensitive skin. Then, see your hands get smoother, whiter, in 12 days!

Change to Ivory for Dishes
See the thick, quick suds pile right up . . . even in hard water! Watch dishes come clean in a hurry! And wonder of wonders, when you look at your hands 12 days from today . . . they'll actually be softer, smoother! Get 3 big bars of Ivory Soap _today_. 99 44/100 % Pure . . . It Floats.

SAVE HANDS...SPEED DISHES

Velvet-suds IVORY SOAP

Advertisements such as this one assured women that they could work and still have nice hands. The woman in the photo, though busy with "war-work plus housework" insisted "there's no excuse for a woman to get slack about dishpan hands." (_Mobile Register_, October 24, 1942; courtesy of Alabama Department of Archives and History) featured in ADDSCO's newsletters were always described as "mighty pretty," "attractive young 'Miss,' " or "fair ladies." In an article, "Worktime and Playtime for Brookley Girls," MoASC's newsletter printed two pictures of the same women, one in their working clothes and another in evening dresses. The article was designed to reassure readers that even though women were engaged in male work they were still women underneath and no change had occurred in traditional sex roles. Both newsletters regularly carried pictures of women employees who had pretty faces and legs. Hence the public's perception of women was unchanged even though they might be engaged in unusual jobs.[35]

The public image of these women may have maintained the prewar cast, but what did these women have to say of themselves? A detailed examination gives a composite, revealing picture of where these women came from and their various reasons for entering the labor force.

The majority of working women came from farms and small towns near the various defense plants in the state. Most employers preferred to hire local people instead of encouraging migrants to move into the area. This was fairly easy to do because, as a result of the Depression, nearly all communities had a labor surplus that was only too willing to work. The one big exception was Mobile, where the labor shortage encouraged migrants to pour into the area in record numbers. They came from the surrounding communities as well as from Mississippi, Georgia, and west Florida. Many women followed their husbands to defense centers as they searched for jobs and often became employed themselves. Mary Cottingham followed this pattern. She moved with her four children from Centreville, Alabama, to Mobile in 1942 to join her husband. She soon secured a job with the Civilian Welfare Association at Brookley Field and eventually became chief clerk.[36]

Younger unmarried women used the boom times as an opportunity to launch a career or to upgrade a current job. Contrary to popular opinion, most women were not strangers to employment. During the 1930s and 1940s, the great majority of women sought and eventually found employment after leaving school. Paid employment before marriage had been the norm in America, although most women left their jobs when they married. Marriage and careers were viewed as incompatible.[37] The experience of some of the women who worked at Brookley Field illustrates the motivation of women who sought employment.

Rowena Reinecke, born and educated in Mobile, worked first as an assistant librarian in the Murphy High School in Mobile and later at the Mobile Drug Company before becoming a secretary at MoASC in 1941. By 1943 she had worked as a secretary for nine officers and was then serving as the secretary to the commanding officer. Carolyn N. Shell grew up on a farm in Monroeville, Alabama, and attended college in Fort Worth, Texas. Her first job was working for the probate judge in Monroe County, then later for the state extension agronomist in Auburn, Alabama. By 1943 she was the chief clerk of the Quartermaster Salvage Section at Brookley Field. She liked that job better than any she ever had. After graduation from high school in Geneva, Alabama, Lillian Sims worked as a bookkeeper in Andalusia until she came to Brookley Field to serve as a receptionist in the Maintenance Division. She liked her job and planned to stay until the war was over, at which time she hoped to marry.[38]

Older married women who had worked before the war were able to secure better positions as a result of wartime prosperity. Approximately one-fourth of all Alabama women were employed in the prewar years, and they were the women who profited most from high-paying formerly male jobs opening up during wartime. These women who had had experience were in a better position than younger, inexperienced women to take advantage of the opportunity offered by the expanding economy. They had skills and knowledge to offer a potential employer, and they had confidence from their previous work experience that made them desirable employees. MoASC employed many such women.

Lois M. Lewis married just before her husband joined the navy in World War I. During that war she worked as a secretary at the Naval Air Station in Pensacola, Florida. She then turned to housekeeping and reared two daughters but returned to work as a buyer for a department store. After World War II started, she went to work at Brookley Field as the chief of the Central File Section. She said: "If you get married young, you can raise your family and all that sort of thing and still have plenty of time left to have a good time. Just because you happen to be a grandmother doesn't mean it's a sign to curl up around the edges." Annie L. Hines, from Grove Hill, Alabama, worked for a hotel for six years before coming to work at MoASC. She was employed as a clerk in the officers' mail room and found that job to be much more interesting. Beulah Clarke was married and had worked for the Coca-Cola Company in Mobile for several years. She was given a leave to work as the secretary of the Housing Division of MoASC.[39]

The wartime economy also provided work opportunities for older women who had never been employed and whose children had left home. These women thought of themselves solely as wives and mothers, but now were motivated to seek paid employment to aid in the war effort. Many of them found the work rewarding. Before coming to Brookley Field, Mauddell D. Mann was a housewife who enjoyed housework and cooking; she also played bridge four times a week. Then she went to work as supervisor of the Maintenance Administration Branch at MoASC and liked her job so well that she hoped to continue it after the war. Elizabeth Sheridan had never worked outside her home until she took a job at the Maintenance Branch of Brookley Field. After a few weeks on the job, she did not want to give it up. After teaching at a school for the deaf and blind, Harriet Gravlee settled down to the business of being a wife and mother. When the war began, she took a job as recreation hostess for Brookley Field, a position at which she was very successful.[40]

A few women had received training in a profession or a skill before the war. They usually worked until they were married or had children. Many of them went back to work because they felt they were needed. Victoria D. Brasell, a native of Mobile, graduated from Bishop Toolen High School and trained as a nurse at Mobile City Hospital. She had retired from nursing when she married, but the urgent need for nurses influenced her to give up housekeeping for the duration and use her special skill in helping the war effort. She became the chief nurse at the Civilian Dispensary at Brookley Field, but she hoped that after the war she could return to keeping house. Elba Wheeler felt much the same way. She had been trained as a secretary at a business school and worked as a stenographer in a newspaper office but left to care for her husband and child. When the war began, she accepted a position with Brookley Field's Quartermaster Corps. She much preferred housekeeping to working but felt that it was her duty to use her clerical training in the war effort.[41]

Many women worked while their husbands were in the armed forces. Some had to work because they could not live on their husbands' pay. Others were motivated to support the war effort until their lovers or husbands came home. Adelaide Touart was a native of Mobile and a graduate of Murphy High School. She kept house for her husband until he went into the army in 1941, when she began to work at Brookley Field as a supervisor in the Civilian Separations Unit. As soon as he returned from India, she hoped to settle down again as a housewife and mother. Vivian Crawford had been employed as a salesperson in New Orleans before the war, but after her husband was sent to Africa, she took a job as a clerk in the Supply Division at Brookley. Ellen H. Mott knew the meaning of war better than others. Her husband had been a prisoner of the Japanese since 1942, when his plane was shot down over Thailand. Mott was a native Mobilian and had attended Gulf Park College in Mississippi. After receiving the news of her husband's capture, she began to work as a secretary at MoASC. "It is hard," she said, "to go month after month without a word from him directly—and I write regularly every week."[42]

Alabama women sought employment for a variety of reasons. War jobs forced them to adapt to a new lifestyle, which included balancing their duties of homemaking and child care with job responsibilities. They often found themselves doing double duty with little help from their husbands or employers. Employers, too, faced new problems. They had to deal with untrained and inexperienced workers. At the beginning of the war, most industries made it clear that they would not hire women until they were absolutely forced to do so. But this reluctance disappeared when it became obvious that a large pool of labor could be tapped by making only a few changes in operating style. As a result, employers began to institute special measures to accommodate women.

Washington Avenue Nursery, Mobile, 1943. (Courtesy of ADDSCO Collection, University of South Alabama Photographic Archives)

CHAPTER 4

Adjusting to

Women Workers

The expansion of the female labor force in Alabama during the war involved more than growth in numbers. It forced changes in the perception of the role of women by management, women themselves, and their male coworkers. In some situations, management was forced to take special measures to accommodate the new employees. Employers realized that women who were hired to fill men's jobs would need to be treated differently from men. Defense contractors were usually willing to make changes because the federal government absorbed the extra expense.

The most common practice was to employ counselors for women. Some companies had employed them before the war, but the practice became widespread when employers had to cope with thousands of new workers who were unfamiliar with the ways of factory life. Counselors' functions were to interpret company rules and regulations to women; to make male workers and foremen more receptive and understanding of women; and to discuss personal problems and assist in obtaining services such as child care, housing, and transportation. The Women's Bureau found that by 1943 almost all factories it surveyed had employed counselors.[1]

Both the Alabama Dry Dock and Shipbuilding Company and the Mobile Air Service Command employed women counselors to assist and support the female employees in their transition into the male work force. ADDSCO began employing counselors in mid-1943, and by early 1944 the staff consisted of nine women headed by Mary McMullen Roberts, a former director of the Mobile County Department of Public Welfare. Roberts and her staff attempted to give women confidence in themselves by providing an introduction and orientation session; explaining company rules and policies; providing information about proper and safe clothing; and assisting workers to find child care facilities, shopping centers, and other community resources.[2]

Roberts knew that both women and men had difficulty adjusting to each other in the shipyard. She acknowledged that the shipyards were not ready for women when they came and asked the men to be supportive of women who were attempting this unusual work. Most counselors concerned themselves with persuading women to dress properly for shipyard work by tying up their long hair and by wearing hard hats, gloves, and safety-toed shoes. Women were even

ADDSCO's women counselors posed for this picture around the desk of their supervisor, Mary McMullen Roberts. "Mary Roberts Discusses Everything from Recipes to Babies to Hairdos with Girl Workers," reported a newspaper headline. Counselors were hired by many war-production companies to explain company regulations to new women employees and provide information on community resources such as child care facilities. (January 1944; courtesy of ADDSCO Collection, University of South Alabama Photographic Archives)

issued an extra ration stamp to buy such shoes. Counselors provided women with information on educational, medical, and recreational facilities. The public was assured that women welders were still interested in feminine topics; a newspaper headline, for example, read "Mary Roberts Discusses Everything from Recipes to Babies to Hairdos with Girl Workers."[3] This view reinforced the understanding that women were taking men's roles only for the duration.

The editors of ADDSCO's newsletter, *Fore & Aft*, realizing that women faced tremendous problems in assuming jobs in industry, established a column devoted solely to women and items of interest to them. The editor of the column, like Mary Roberts, was concerned with encouraging women to tie up and cover their long hair. Women were supposed to wear bandanas or turbans over their hair at all times. One worker, Della Fulghum, got tired of this method of hair covering and made a snood from an old window curtain, which she described as easy to make and comfy to wear. If a woman wanted to brighten up her coveralls for spring, she could get checked or plain material and make a dickey and a head handkerchief to match. Another worker, Florence Johnson, made her own coveralls out of bed ticking; they were described as comfortable and easy to launder. Women were constantly being reminded of the necessity of wearing safety-toed shoes. These were seen as "surprisingly good looking and . . . strong and safe, and cheap and unrationed." Women workers could buy these shoes at cost. Advice was also given about how to clean the dirt and grease from fingernails.[4]

Both the government and employees soon recognized that if they wanted to increase the labor supply and reduce absenteeism, they would have to address the dual responsibilities of female workers. Employed women during the war found themselves carrying double burdens as working women always had. In addition to their paid war work, they remained the principal homemakers for their families. Wartime brought the first real recognition of this double role, and some attempts were made to help women with these obligations. Shortages of food, consumer goods, transportation, and medical care made combining paid employment with domestic duties even more difficult. The government publicized the problems and encouraged business and communities to expand shopping hours and inaugurate prepared food services to ease the burden on women.

In July 1942, the stores of Birmingham extended their shopping hours until 9:00 P.M. on Mondays and to 6:00 P.M. other days. Birmingham was the first city in the state to institute such a change, which at the time was viewed as revolutionary. Instead of the traditional 9:30 to 5:30, business establishments began in July 1942 to open at noon on Mondays and remain open until 9:00 P.M. On the other days of the week the stores remained opened until 6:00 P.M., except on Saturday, when the hours were extended to 7:00 P.M. Providing longer shopping hours in the evening was designed to lighten the load on public transportation during rush hours and also to give defense workers more time to do their shopping.[5]

Traditions died harder in Mobile. It was not until April 1943 that Mobile merchants began to stay open longer hours. The Chamber of Commerce together with representatives of the army, the War Manpower Commission, and the larger industries of the city appealed to merchants to remain open Monday evenings until 9:00 to allow war workers to shop at a time that did not conflict with their employment hours. The president of the Chamber of Commerce, Judge Ben D. Turner, appealed to the patriotism of local businessmen. The WMC, Brookley Field authorities, and officials of the two shipyards presented evidence that many men and women were taking time off from their jobs to shop. "We urge, as a means of patriotically helping to meet this absenteeism problem, that all merchants keep their stores closed until 12:30 noon on Mondays, then open and remain open until 9 P.M.," declared Judge Turner.[6] All retail stores, public utilities, barber shops, and other service establishments adjusted their hours, although banks, drugstores, laundries, and dry cleaners maintained the old schedules.

This plan met the needs of employed women. One female employee at Brookley said, "This plan is really a Godsend to us. . . . Up to now I could never get to the stores before 5:15 P.M. and never had time to do all the shopping I planned. Last week I went on

Monday evening and had plenty of time to shop at my leisure and get everything I needed." The USES observed an immediate 25 percent drop in absenteeism, from 12 to 9 percent. This adjustment in hours was effective not only because it gave workers time after work to shop but also because workers had no place to go with the stores closed Monday mornings and consequently returned to work. Merchants also benefited because, with more time, women were able to buy more. The success of the plan was evident because the stores were as crowded as they would be on the day before Christmas. They were so crowded that Mary Roberts made a plea for people who could shop during the day to avoid shopping on Monday nights.[7]

The most critical problem that women faced was that of child care. The government approached this problem with ambivalence. The WMC discouraged mothers with small children from working in defense plants: "Now as in peacetime, a mother's primary duty is to her home and children." Secretary of Labor Frances Perkins and Mary Anderson of the Women's Bureau believed that this duty could not be laid aside even during wartime. Because of this attachment to traditional ideas of women's role, the federal government was hesitant to create child care centers for women employed in defense work. Officials recognized, however, that some mothers had to work from financial necessity and that in some areas labor shortages were sufficiently severe that employment of mothers was necessary.

In 1943 some $400,000 was allotted under the authority of the Lanham Act to establish day care centers, a totally inadequate sum to provide care for children of war workers. Federal and local day care programs served only 10 percent of the nation's working mothers. Even when centers were established, women often chose not to place their children in them, either because they were associated with welfare or because they were not well administered. As a result, American women did not have the family service and housekeeping assistance that British women enjoyed, and American women shouldered an extra burden on behalf of their country in time of crisis.[8]

The view of Alabamians toward working mothers was expressed in *Alabama Social Welfare,* a monthly journal published by the State Department of Public Welfare:

> It is generally accepted that because of the importance of the conservation of home and family life, employment policies should include due consideration at every point to the responsibilities of women as mothers. While in our total war effort it would be inconceivable to place absolute barriers against the employment of mothers with young children, such mothers should not be actively recruited as a new source of labor until other sources of labor supply in the communities have been fully utilized, and employment practices should take the home responsibilities of mothers so recruited into consideration.[9]

Despite this ambivalence, Alabama authorities did attempt to address the problem of child care.

In early 1942, the director of the State Department of Public Welfare, Loula Dunn, became concerned with the need for day care facilities for children whose mothers were employed in essential war activities. None of the areas affected had adequate public or private child care facilities, and it was immediately obvious that steps would need to be taken. Instances were reported of girls as young as ten or twelve taking full charge of younger children during the day. School-age children were left without supervision in the afternoons. One mill owner said that from fourteen to twenty-four of his women employees were absent each day because there was no one to look out after their children at home. The Public Welfare Department felt that these problems were national in scope and no community could meet them alone. The question, as the department saw it, was not whether women should be employed for industrial work but how to meet the needs of the children when their mothers were employed.[10]

By October 1942, the State Advisory Committee on Day Care had been established. It recommended the appointment of local advisory committees to organize community day care centers. Dunn believed that the need for such care would not be confined to welfare families but would include families who could pay the entire cost of child care. The State Advisory Committee recommended the establishment of additional day care facilities in seventeen Alabama communities. Dunn estimated that between twenty-five hundred and three thousand children needed day care while their mothers were working in vital defense industries. Nineteen day care centers were already functioning in these seventeen communities, but Dunn believed that thirty more were needed.[11]

The possibility of fathers sharing child care responsibilities was never seriously considered. Dunn, writing in *Alabama Social Welfare*, reflected the prevailing view of the times toward the distribution of labor between men and women at home:

> A married man who has to be at his factory at seven o'clock in the morning has presumably little to do before he goes to work. While he may not get home before seven o'clock, again he has little to do other than eat his supper and go to bed. On the other hand a married woman employed with children who has to get to work by seven o'clock, has also to get the children up, prepare the younger ones to go to the day care center (if there be one) and the older ones for school. She presumably cooks the breakfast for the family, takes the pre-school age children to the center and then goes to work. Whether she gets home at five o'clock or seven o'clock, she has to see that the children are home and prepare their evening meal after leaving her work. It is plain that the married working woman with children has at least four or five hours essential work to do apart from her work at the factory.[12]

The option of redistribution of labor between men and women was not seriously considered.

The only available nurseries in the state in 1942 were those supported by the Works Progress Administration. During the Depression the WPA had established nurseries as a welfare measure to provide jobs for teachers as well as to provide care for children of welfare families. Despite the need for child care after the war began, these nurseries were not used to capacity because of the stigma of welfare attached to them. The State Department of Public Welfare and the USES became convinced that other facilities would have to be established. The WPA funds expired in early 1943 and were not renewed. After a brief delay, President Roosevelt ruled that Lanham Act funds for the construction of wartime facilities could be used to build and operate day care centers. This act was a bureaucratic maze that involved matching funds and was administered by the Federal Works Administration (FWA).[13]

Mobile was the area of greatest congestion as well as the area of largest female employment, so it was most in need of child care centers. The only available nurseries in the county when the first recruitment drive to employ women was held in September 1942 were those built by the WPA. At that time, six of these nurseries were operating with an enrollment of 125 children. With an anticipated increase in the numbers of women working, these day care centers expanded their list of eligible children to include those of working mothers and those whose fathers were in the armed forces or engaged in defense work. The number of children did not greatly increase, however, even though the centers could accommodate 200, because women did not want to use facilities that were associated with welfare. The USES was convinced that other facilities would have to be made available if women were to be successfully recruited. After the WPA funds expired in early 1943, the day care centers in Mobile closed for a brief period and then reopened contingent upon securing matching funds under the Lanham Act.[14]

By June 1943, Mobile had opened eight nurseries with facilities for 550 children and anticipated opening four others. To operate the eight nurseries, $13,000 in local funds had yet to be raised. Six of these centers were for white children and two for black. By fees from parents and donations from war industries, the necessary money was raised by July 4, at which time the city announced it had been granted $47,050 from Lanham funds. The total cost of the Mobile project was $87,398, of which the school board contributed $40,348. The grant was designed to operate twelve nurseries that would accommodate 615 children. These nurseries would care for children aged two to six whose mothers worked in war plants or whose fathers were in the armed forces. The nursery supervisor was Lillian Poyntz, who had been educated at the University of Minnesota and had been in charge of the WPA nurseries.[15]

In addition to these nurseries for preschool children, the city established two day care centers for children aged six to twelve. The program was first organized and run by the Parent Teachers Association (PTA) in August 1943, then was taken over in October by the nursery school program. These day care centers provided supervision for school-age children before and after school and on Saturdays. The purpose of the program was to keep the children off the streets and give them the care they would receive at home, thereby preventing juvenile delinquency. One observer said the children arrived early and stayed late, but all of them were good soldiers.[16]

It was not until March 1943 that Birmingham inaugurated a drive for child care facilities. At that time a group of women from various community organizations including the PTA, Junior League, WPA nursery schools, and others met to devise a plan to establish child care centers for the children of the increasing number of working women. These plans got nowhere because the WPA funds were not renewed. In May 1943, however, both the city of Birmingham and the county applied for and received money from the Lanham Act. The city received $35,798 to build thirteen nurseries to be operated under the authority of the Board of Education. These Lanham funds had to be matched by local money, which in Birmingham was supplied by various local agencies. The county received $54,530 to build seven nursery units, five preschool units, and twelve extended-school-day units for older children. At the same time Bessemer received $5,649, Montgomery County $22,810, and Gadsden $11,000.[17]

Despite the relatively large number of child care centers available, they were seldom filled to capacity because only a small number of mothers used their services. By November 1943, facilities were available in Mobile for 400 children, but the average attendance was only 185. In October 1944 the number of children enrolled had increased to 444, but the capacity had risen to 680.[18] The USES attempted to increase enrollment by providing information to personnel officers of war industries and by promoting newspaper publicity showing favorable conditions in the centers.[19] The majority of working mothers, however, chose to seek alternatives to group care, for a wide variety of reasons. Conditions at these centers were often less than desirable, and women frequently chose to leave their children with a family member or with someone they knew and trusted. In Mobile overt hostility was expressed toward working mothers who left their children at day care facilities. In June 1943 several mothers were told bluntly by protesting women that they should stay home to care for their children. As Susan Hartmann has pointed out, "Given a public consensus that working mothers were at best a necessary evil and that children were better off with individual nurturance, women's resistance to group care is not surprising."[20] Indeed, partially filled centers were common across the nation.

Prejudice against working women did diminish somewhat during the war, at least as long as their labor was felt to be necessary for the war effort. Initially the War Manpower Commission preferred to recruit single women, but when that supply was exhausted, married women were sought. The belief stemming from the Depression that married women were depriving male breadwinners of jobs was less convincing with the wartime labor shortage. Despite the proclamation by the media that "it's up to the married women" to take defense jobs, married women with children faced the greatest social disapproval. Public opinion was reflected in the government's policy of discouraging mothers of young children from working. Working mothers became an easy scapegoat as juvenile delinquency increased. The charge was made that mothers might win the war on the production line but lose it on the home front.[21]

When the war began, Alabamians appeared to support the concept of women working in the defense industries. The public and the newspapers supported the recruitment drives, and women war workers were glorified as heroines. Women who aided in the war effort were lauded for their patriotism. The great concern of public officials was to provide day care centers for these working mothers. For a short period women were viewed primarily as workers, not solely as wives and mothers. But by mid-1943 this brief flirtation with new roles for women came to an end. Instead of being concerned with child care, public attention was directed to juvenile delinquency. Articles about delinquent children and disrupted families began to dominate the newspaper pages. The common themes were the needs of children in wartime and the effect of the war on the family, implying that the employment of women was largely to blame: "Let us do our utmost to see that all man-power is utilized . . . before we take the mothers of young children out of the home. Let us prevent rather than contribute to the growth of juvenile delinquency. We already have proof of what can happen to children when both parents are working outside the home."[22]

Citizens in many Alabama communities, especially Mobile and Birmingham, began to see a link between women's wartime role and increased problems with youth. This new attitude was summed up in the newspaper headline "Mothers Busy at Work, Youth Easily Strays into Delinquency." A group of concerned citizens organized the Jefferson County Youth Protective Association to combat juvenile delinquency during the 1943 summer vacation. The director suggested that mothers be given flexible working hours and appealed to industries to arrange split shifts or shorter hours for working mothers so they could be with their children during the summer months. She commented, "Frankly, it seems to us that mothers who choose to give up jobs rather than neglect their children are contributing as much to the war effort as they would be making air planes and leaving their children at loose ends to become a responsibility to the community and likely delinquents."[23]

Later that same summer, some five hundred citizens of Birmingham met at the Tutwiler Hotel and formed the Juvenile Protective Association, which was concerned with the prevention and control of juvenile delinquency. One speaker declared that more emphasis should be placed on how to live than on how to make a living. Many suggestions were made to handle the problem; one was that women should return home and care for their children.[24]

Mobile was equally concerned with the problems of juveniles. As early as January 1943, newspaper articles and editorials expressed concern about juvenile delinquency. By June citizens were told that "juvenile delinquency is the problem of each and every Mobilian." In October 1943, editorials were expressing concern over the effect of working mothers on child care and making a connection with rising juvenile delinquency. One editorial quoted an FBI official who related rising rates of delinquency among girls to lack of supervision in the home and community.[25]

The solution proposed by Mobile authorities was to establish a curfew. The county probation officer, who favored the curfew, believed that delinquency developed in homes with both fathers and mothers working. The city commission considered the proposal but did not adopt it because of opposition. Citizens pointed out that a curfew would not get to the root of the problem; it would not command respect for the law on the part of children, and it would be a law for the few, with law-abiding children, who formed the majority, paying the penalty.[26]

The juveniles who were causing the most concern were young girls, who were described as being attracted by military camps and high-paying war plants. Such girls were "a bad influence" in any community, and parents were encouraged to observe closely their daughters' associates. The "girl problem" was especially acute around army posts, and delinquency was developing even among girls under the age of twelve. Law enforcement officers in Montgomery said, "We used to have trouble with regular prostitutes; now our problem is these young girls." Grand juries in both Jefferson and Mobile counties urged closer control of young girls as a step in preventing juvenile delinquency. These juries believed that parents were lax in the supervision of daughters, allowing them to associate with soldiers and civilians "day and night making contacts in places of questionable character, and having no knowledge of the dangers these girls are facing."[27]

Condemnation of working women was more open and expressed more often in Mobile than elsewhere in the state. The question of working married women was viewed as a moral rather than an economic issue. The U.S. Employment Service in Mobile attempted to carry out the WMC's mandate to recruit women but ran into "religious" objections to female employment. The attitude of Mobilians was probably no different from that of other Alabamians, but because Mobile experienced greater social dislocation than any other area, these common feelings were more openly expressed.[28]

Opposition to working mothers was expressed by many in Mobile, but by no one more influential than Bishop Thomas J. Toolen of the Roman Catholic Diocese of Mobile-Birmingham. Toolen arrived in Mobile in 1927 and revitalized the diocese. By World War II he was one of the town's most powerful leaders. The bishop acknowledged that the government had asked women to enter war work, but he expressed the commonly held view, "What good would it be to win this war on foreign battle fields and lose it at home? A woman can do much more for her country by staying at home and raising her children to be law-abiding, God-fearing citizens than she can in any war industry." Toolen felt that greed was the chief reason why women took war jobs. He said, "They have seen all the money floating by and they want their share."[29]

The bishop did support women's presence in the armed forces, although when he first heard about it, he was shocked. He became reconciled to the idea in the face of the grave national emergency, assuming that when these women came home again, they would be better wives and mothers as a result of the work they had done for their country. He likened them to Joan of Arc.[30]

Other Mobilians were not so willing to blame women for the social problems that arose. One who disagreed with Bishop Toolen was the Reverend Ansley C. Moore of the Government Street Presbyterian Church, who defended working mothers: "Some who have spoken publicly on these matters . . . are now denouncing the women who have taken war jobs for their greed when everybody three months ago here was begging our women to lend industry a hand. Condemning this woman for greed and laying the entire problem of child delinquency at her door is . . . defeating our national emergency program."[31]

Others also objected to putting all the blame on mothers. E. B. Bowman, chairman of the Juvenile Court Commission, said: "It requires a deeper understanding to sense the motives which prompt many mothers to go into war industries. They, too, feel the patriotic urge to do something. They see an opportunity to earn money and pay off old debts. They see a college education for 'junior' in the weekly envelope. Not all working mothers are neglecting their children." An editorial pointed out that "working mothers have been in American life for an untold period of years and have brought forth some of the best families."[32]

Married women who took wartime jobs were caught in a conflict. The federal government encouraged women to work in defense industries or take service or office jobs; when they did, however, they were viewed as greedy and neglecting their duties as wives and mothers. Despite the unprecedented opportunity for employment, the majority of women during the 1940s had no career aspirations and saw their primary role in life as that of homemaker and mother. The war did not cause a drastic break with traditional working patterns or sex roles. As we have seen, the recruitment effort was intended by the government and perceived by the public as a temporary expedient to last only for the duration of the war. Women worked because they needed the money to support themselves or someone else. There is no indication that their primary interest in the home decreased. Alabamians, like other Americans, were fearful of a change in traditional sex roles, but despite increased female employment men were still viewed as breadwinners and women as homemakers. Nevertheless, not all women wanted to abandon their jobs when the war was over.

By mid-1944 the courtship of women by the federal government came to an end. Its span was shorter than the war itself. Groups that had urged women to take advantage of war jobs rolled up the welcome mat. Americans united to thank the women who had contributed to victory but assumed that women would return to their homes when the war was over. There was widespread fear that the end of defense production and the release of millions of American soldiers would bring about an economic depression. A partial solution to this problem would be the retirement of millions of women workers to domesticity. Hence when labor scarcity turned to surplus, employers resumed their preference for male workers, supported by the continuing assumption that men should be the breadwinners. This desire to employ men was further reinforced by veterans' legal and moral claims to employment. Earlier, women had been told it was their patriotic duty to work; now the argument was that it was their patriotic duty to go back to the kitchen and let veterans have their jobs. Women were once again called on to change their roles to conform to the nation's economic needs.[33]

By the end of 1946, two million women had left the labor force and another million were laid off. The proportion of women who were employed dropped from 36 percent at the war's end to 28 percent in 1947. This decline nearly wiped out all the gains women had made during the war years. The woman worker was no longer a symbol of patriotism but a threat to social and economic security.[34]

Most Mobile women were able to keep their jobs until the early months of 1945. Alabama Dry Dock and Shipbuilding Company began massive layoffs in February 1945. By August thirteen thousand workers had been discharged. The percentage of women employed dropped from a high of 11.6 in December 1944 to 8 in July 1945. By May 1946, the figure had fallen to 3 percent; shipbuilding was essentially an exclusively all-male field once again.[35]

As the women were laid off from their jobs, they were praised for their work. A picture captioned "Last All Girl Welding Crew on Shipways" appeared in ADDSCO's newsletter with the statement that supervisors were proud of the crew and believed the "girls" had done "a swell job." The second-shift superintendent of the burners complimented the "women who have been 'pinch-hitting' for the boys who are fighting for the freedom of America."[36] Again it was made clear that women's employment was only temporary.

The percentage of women at the Mobile Air Service Command dropped somewhat more slowly. As late as May 1945, MoASC still employed 48 percent women, approximately the same as at the height of the war. A year later the figure was 31 percent. The USES stated in November 1946 that there would be practically no expansion in female employment. Women could no longer anticipate acquiring high-paying defense jobs and instead would seek employment in other areas such as food services, pulp and paper mills, service institutions, and retail trade.[37]

The Bechtel-McCone-Parsons plant in Birmingham began laying off workers after the war ended in Europe in May 1945. The sharpest contract cancellations, however, occurred in August, when forty-nine hundred people were released. In that month the maximum unemployment was listed as four thousand, which included about twenty-five hundred women for whom there were no job opportunities. The USES reasoned that since comparatively few women were engaged in production work before the war, the majority of them would retire when jobs were no longer available. Women were expected to return to their homes or perhaps to their former occupations.[38]

But the war worker could not be cast off like an old glove. Many working women were glad to return home, but others were working because they needed the money to support their families. Women were mature, adult members of society who could and did make their own decisions. The stated preference of many for employment was generally ignored. In the nation as a whole, half the women who were out of work in 1947 were actively seeking jobs. Some found them at lower pay; some stayed in white-collar clerical jobs; others joined the long-term unemployed on welfare rolls. The women who wanted and needed jobs had to find work in less skilled and less highly paid occupations. After spending the war years in men's jobs, they were back to "women's work." For working-class women nationwide, the end of the war meant a promise withdrawn just as it seemed about to be fulfilled.[39]

The attitudes of Alabama women toward continuing employment varied greatly. Many women did look forward to retiring and returning to being full-time wives and mothers. Lillie Mae Pratt, who worked as a civilian guard at Brookley Field, said: "I've been married

long enough to know that a housewife's work never ends, neverthe-less I much prefer dishwashing and housework to doing a man's job."
Mary Cottingham, chief clerk of the Civilian Welfare Association, said that when the war was over she wanted to move back to the family farm in Bibb County and keep house for her four growing children and her husband: "When that day comes the family can be sure of being served country fried chicken several times a week." Irene F. Ramsey, who moved to Mobile from Memphis to work in the airplane repair section, said: "I plan to keep house for my hus-band wherever he decides to settle down. . . . I don't plan to work outside the home."[40]

The commonly held view regarding postwar employment for women was summed up in a headline in the *Welfarer,* which read: "Soldiers Welcome to Our Jobs, Say MoASC Women: These Work-ers Will Gladly Give up Wartime Careers for Home and Family." The article went on to say that the much discussed battle of the sexes would be a fizzle because a cross-section of women interviewed wanted to return home. These women were more interested in marriage, babies, washing machines and vacuum cleaners than in wartime jobs: "GI Joe should come marching back from the wars into his peacetime job without any competition from the ladies interviewed." A closer reading of the responses of women inter-viewed revealed that half wanted to return to domestic life, but the other half had career goals in mind.[41] The author of the article seems to have reflected the widely held view without considering carefully what women themselves were saying.

A substantial number of women found their jobs a decided im-provement over unpaid housework. Gladys Brodbeck, assistant supervisor of housing at Brookley Field, said she hoped to obtain a permanent civil service job so she could stay on at Brookley because she had come to love her work. Mauddell D. Mann, supervisor of the Maintenance Administration Branch, was a housewife before the war who played bridge several times a week, but at the war's end she wanted to keep her job. Several other women expressed an interest in continuing to work in civil service positions. After working with the air command one employee wanted to be an airline stewardess and others hoped for careers as pilots.[42] Many of those who anticipated working were older women whose children were grown. Brookley employed several hundred women who were grandmothers in their fifties; all these women preferred to stay on in their wartime jobs rather than return to domesticity.

National polls showed that 61 to 85 percent of women workers wanted to keep their jobs.[43] The Women's Bureau surveyed the ten congested defense centers and found that an average of 75 percent of the women employed in 1944–45 planned to continue working.[44] In Mobile 84 percent of the women desired continued employment; this figure indicated that three times as many women wanted to work as were employed in 1940. Almost all black women planned to continue to work and 79 percent of white women expressed this desire.[45] The majority of these women had little choice because they had to support themselves or others.

During the war, Alabama industries and public officials made attempts to change the conditions under which women worked. Employers hired special counselors for women who aided them in adjusting to factory life; attempts were made to address women's dual responsibilities by extending shopping hours and providing child care facilities. Prejudice against married women working abated during the early years, but it surfaced again by mid-1943 as public concern over juvenile delinquency increased. Working mothers were easy scapegoats for social problems. By mid-1944 women were being encouraged to return to the home and make way for the returning veterans. Some women, however, desired to continue working; their wishes were largely disregarded.

CHAPTER 5

Women and

Volunteer Activities

Not all Alabama women followed in the footsteps of Rosie the Riveter and sought paying jobs in defense plants. Because only a little more than a third of all women were employed, the majority continued their prewar roles as students, wives, homemakers, and mothers. These women, were, however, encouraged by the government to engage in volunteer work. The federal government attempted to bolster morale and speed up mobilization by encouraging women to devote their energies to war-related tasks. The Office of Civilian Defense (OCD) organized air raid wardens, auxiliary police, and nurses' aides. The OCD gave a "V Home Award" to families who made "themselves into a fighting unit on the homefront" by conserving food, salvaging scrap, buying war bonds, and refusing to hoard scarce commodities. The smallest act, such as deciding not to buy something, was viewed as aiding the war effort. Whole communities joined together in the war effort by planting gardens in vacant lots and conducting drives for fats, papers, and rubber.[1]

For the majority of Americans, World War II did not bring suffering but rather an improved standard of living. Full employment and high earnings were in sharp contrast with the Depression of the 1930s. As a result of wartime prosperity, the United States entered the longest period of economic growth in its history. Even by 1943 seven out of ten Americans could say that the war had not required them to make any real sacrifices, a claim few people in Britain, France, or Russia could make. Instead, Americans often felt satisfaction in contributing to the common good. Those on the home front had a greater opportunity to provide valuable service than in previous wars. Participation in a common cause tended to enhance each person's sense of worth and promote feelings of comradeship and well-being.

Volunteer activity in officially approved war programs occupied the leisure time of about one-fourth of all American women. Participation varied by age, class, and race. Housewives in their thirties and forties were the most active, whereas the mothers of young children, older women, and workers had less time, energy, and opportunity to contribute. Middle-class women who had had some college training were much more likely to volunteer than women from less privileged backgrounds. More educated women had had experience with organized social activities outside the home and had learned the skills necessary to work effectively. War-related activities at the local level were set up and run through established clubs and organizations, with middle-class women as the voluntary leaders and organizers.[2] Black women also offered their volunteer services in their communities and various organizations. Many of them were as civic-minded as white women in supporting the war bond drives, the Red Cross, and the USO.

The Civilian Defense Program was the first and most prominent organization that sought the aid of volunteers. The federal government established the Office of Civilian Defense even before the war began under the direction of Fiorello LaGuardia, mayor of New York City. By November 1941 all states, including Alabama, had set up defense councils, which were authorized to create a Citizens' Defense Corps. These volunteers acted as air raid wardens, auxiliary firemen, emergency medical corps, nurses' aides, and messengers. A model defense council plan was prepared by the ODC, and many states followed it in establishing their own civilian defense; but ODC officials never had the power to enforce their policies. The result

YOU CAN HELP BUILD THIS BOMBER!

"It may sound funny to hear a girl like me say that you can help build a bomber—but it's true just the same.

"It takes *thousands* of long distance telephone calls to build one of these giant bombers—calls to every part of the country, and for many reasons, from changing blueprint plans to speeding the delivery of parts. These long distance calls are as important to you as they are to us who help build these ships of the skies.

"To help speed the building of more bombers, ships and guns, won't you please make only the most necessary long distance calls and be brief on all calls. In this way you will definitely help us war workers and our men at the front who need more and more of all kinds of war materials.

"The next time you reach for your telephone to make a long distance call, won't you please remember our plea for your help, and not call unless you really have to."

MAKE FEWER CALLS

Materials needed to build new telephone lines are now going to war. So to serve the greatest number of people with the equipment we have, we need to make fewer calls and be brief on all calls.

Long distance lines to these cities are especially crowded with war calls. Make only really urgent calls to these points or to places in these general localities.

CHICAGO	DETROIT	MEMPHIS	PENSACOLA
CINCINNATI	KNOXVILLE	NASHVILLE	PHILADELPHIA
DALLAS	LOUISVILLE	NEW YORK	ST. LOUIS

Housewives were encouraged to feel that they could contribute to the war effort, even "help build a bomber" at least indirectly, by making fewer long-distance calls. Telephone lines were generally inadequate to meet heavy wartime demands for long-distance communication. (*Birmingham News*, May 3, 1943; courtesy of Alabama Department of Archives and History)

was that enforcement of regulations and penalties for violation were carried out through state laws or municipal ordinances.[3]

In Alabama, Governor Frank Dixon appointed the State Defense Council in January 1941 composed of representatives of such interest groups as agriculture, civil protection, health, welfare, education, housing, human resources, industrial relations, and consumer interests. Houston Cole was named as the first director in 1941; he was followed by Haygood Paterson in 1942. During the last year of the war, from June 1944 to May 1945, the council published a monthly bulletin, *Home Front,* which described the war bond drives, the salvage drives, the used clothing drives, the recruitment drives for WACS and WAVES, and other war-related activities.[4]

The governor also appointed a defense council for each county, which was expected to put together local civilian defense programs. These local councils were responsible for preparing the community to protect itself in event of attack and also for coordinating all community war-related activities. To accomplish this goal, the local councils established Civilian Defense Volunteer Offices as clearing-houses for the entire defense effort in the community. The purpose of these offices was to mobilize all civilian war efforts by providing volunteers with information on how their services could best be used. Women staffed these offices in local communities, but the commanders of the county defense councils were all men with one exception. Mrs. Fred Smith offered her services to the ODC in Montgomery when it asked for "competent men" and was appointed commander of Baldwin County. She completed the necessary training and established a Defense Corps Center with air raid wardens, fire fighters, repair crews, and messengers.[5]

The combat division of civilian defense held air raid drills and mock bombing raids in several Alabama cities. Three such raids were conducted in Birmingham during 1942 and 1943. The most ambitious and successful one was held in May 1943, when thirty-eight Civil Air Patrol (CAP) planes dropped ten thousand "bombs" in fifteen minutes on the area from Leeds to Hueytown. These bombs, which schoolchildren had filled with flour, "hit" Boy Scouts, who lay covered with ketchup while workers gave mock first aid. During this raid, which lasted two hours, forty thousand civilians stood guard to protect property. Colonel R. M. Nolan, military adviser for the Jefferson County Defense Council, said, "If anything we were over-manned for a Sunday afternoon's raid." At Elyton Village and Smith-field Court, government housing projects in Birmingham's west end, five hundred green-streamered gas bombs were dropped. Some seven hundred people were evacuated to Legion Field, where the Red Cross had established a temporary shelter. Captain John Atkin-son announced, "We now have a communications system more than adequate for any emergency that might arise." Blacks demanded the right to participate in these drills and practices; they especially wanted the right to patrol their own neighborhoods, but they never were included in the program.[6]

Civil defense officials also conducted bomb reconnaissance schools in Birmingham, Mobile, and Montgomery to teach carefully selected defense workers how to handle bombs. These two-day courses were held in Birmingham and Mobile during August 1942 and in Mont-gomery during November of the same year. Officers from the U.S. Army Ordnance Department and the Bomb Disposal School of the Aberdeen Proving Grounds in Maryland conducted the classes. One air raid warden from each county was trained as a bomb reconnais-sance expert to determine the presence or absence of bombs during and after air raids. "The importance of this school cannot be over-emphasized," said Colonel Nolan. "We are, therefore, selecting persons who will be benefited by the course and who, in turn, will be of benefit to the community in the event of disaster from bombs."[7]

These volunteer activities dealing with protection from air raids and bomb disposal were dominated by men because few women were air raid wardens during the early years of the war. A special program was held in Birmingham during this period, however, to instruct women on the proper course of action during an air raid. The senior air raid warden of Jefferson County conducted this meet-ing, in cooperation with the auxiliary police and firemen, to instruct women and others not connected with civilian defense.[8]

One area of civilian defense that was eventually dominated by women was the Ground Observer Corps (GOC). The army organized a network of observation posts along the coastal areas of the country, which were operated by the GOC of the Army Air Forces Aircraft Warning Service. Corps members were civilians who were stationed in aircraft spotter posts along both coasts. Their function was to report every plane in the sky to the army's Filter Centers, which were located in major coastal cities. The Filter Centers determined the status of the planes and would relay warnings, if necessary, to the appropriate civilian defense control points. These spotters had to spend many lonely hours in observation posts, scanning the skies. Before the war, the War Department hoped for an "army of 500,000 with each post manned by 19 men in good physical condition." But as the war progressed, women and youths were employed in increasing numbers. At its peak the GOC mobilized six hundred thousand citizens nationally, many of whom were rural and farm people. By keeping track of all the planes in the area, these spotters put an end to false reports of enemy planes and made it unlikely that an unidentified friendly plane could trigger a full-scale alert.[9]

In Alabama, spotters were stationed at Mobile, Bay Minette, Flomaton, Foley, Butler, and Bayou La Batre. The spotters had to learn to judge how far away a plane was, how many engines it had, and how high it was flying. When a plane was spotted, the observer informed the Aircraft Warning Service with the words "Army Flash." Only women were available for this volunteer service because of the tremendous labor shortage in the shipbuilding area of Mobile. The regional commander of the Aircraft Warning Service, Major Isaac Molella, conducted many recruitment drives to encourage women between the ages of eighteen and fifty to serve as spotters. He had reasonable success because in January 1943, 295 women were presented with wings for their aircraft warning work. Some of them performed their duties under difficult circumstances. Mrs. Herbert Lunsford in Foley faithfully remained on duty during an epidemic of the mumps until the other observers were again able to take their turn. Mrs. F. S. Fabre of Mobile worked as a spotter in addition to keeping house for her ten children, most of whom worked at different hours because they, too, had wartime jobs. She commented, "Women are needed and I think they should give up everything necessary to win. It makes me feel so much better to be able to write my soldier son that I am all out for victory like he is."[10]

The volunteer services of the women of Alabama were further used by the Office of Civilian Defense with the establishment of the Citizens' Service Corps (SCS), an agency of the OCD. The SCS, an organization of all service agencies, attempted to bring together community leaders who were willing to give time and effort to such war service programs as Victory gardens; salvage campaigns; Victory speakers, who delivered canned talks on various government policies; block leaders, who informed their neighbors about various war-related programs; car pools; and preinduction counseling for draftees. The corps provided service groups with a voice in community defense activities and identified volunteers. The SCS was an important part of the home front with specific jobs that fit women's abilities and needs.[11] Black women were not included in the SCS program.

The first Citizens' Service Corps was established in Montgomery in October 1942, and by January 1943 the CSC had registered approximately 614 men and women and 262 had been given assignments in civilian defense. Mrs. Silas D. Cater was employed as full-time director. The corps conducted a scrap metal drive, which grew from a small beginning of seventy tons to nearly seven thousand tons. Women collected fats from homes at the rate of a thousand pounds per month. They also worked with the USO and the Travelers' Aid Society to help the men stationed at Maxwell and Gunter fields. The corps supported the Block Plan, through which the housewives of Montgomery organized block leaders to dispense information about salvage, nutrition, war bonds, and other defense measures.[12]

In June 1943 the Citizens' Service Corps in Birmingham launched a massive drive to survey the womanpower in the area. The city was the first in the Fourth Service Command to be selected by the War Department for such a survey. The corps, assisted by a contingent of WACS, determined the numbers, talents, and skills of all women over the age of twenty. The WACS worked in Birmingham for two weeks before moving to another city to conduct a similar survey. Local businesses ran advertisements encouraging women to cooperate in the survey by saying: "The OCD workers are your neighbors, women who are voluntarily giving their time to this work. They will deliver a survey questionnaire to your home, and collect it later, after it has been answered. You will cooperate, won't you?" The results were forwarded to the War Department to use in whatever manner appeared appropriate. It is difficult to think of any practical use for such a survey except to provide jobs for the WACS and the CSC volunteers.[13]

The Birmingham CSC did engage in a number of practical activities to aid the war effort. Some women, who were called the Bundles for America Group, made bathrobes for servicemen to be used at the USO center. Others in the same group made layettes for babies of the wives of servicemen in the Birmingham area. High school girls made scrapbooks of old magazines for the men at the Army Air Base hospital. The CSC furnished hundreds of volunteers for the Office of Price Administration to assist in mailing more than three million ration books. More than five hundred high school students, as well as fifty girls from the Girls Training School, aided in this job. Other CSC women made weekly visits to the grocery stores to determine whether prices were in keeping with OPA guidelines. Many of those who worked with the CSC were middle-aged women whose sons were serving in the armed forces. Mrs. George L. Bailes, CSC director, had a son who served in the air corps. Another clubwoman, Mrs. M. F. Moreland, had a son in the army and a daughter in the WACS. Mrs. J. W. Bradshaw, staff assistant at the CSC volunteer office, came to work even after she received the news that her son was missing in action over North Africa. These women had always done volunteer work, but this time it was aimed at promoting the war effort on the home front.[14]

Those Alabama women who did not volunteer for the Citizens' Service Corps could and did volunteer for the Red Cross. The Red

Red Cross worker with convalescing servicemen in Birmingham. (Courtesy
of Archives and Manuscripts, Birmingham Public Library)

Cross established training programs for nurses' aides, which were
badly needed because of the shortage of nurses. Other women spent
a day a week rolling bandages or knitting and sewing for the Red
Cross; still others worked as Grey Ladies, served in the Canteen
Corps, or chauffeured for the Motor Corps. The U.S. Cadet Nurse
Corps attracted young girls into nursing. The Red Cross appealed
to middle- and upper-class women who were accustomed to club
work; this was one way that mothers, wives, and daughters could do
something to help their loved ones in the armed forces. They could
not directly help their men, but the Red Cross could and did. Black
women in Birmingham, Tuskegee, and Mobile established their own
chapters of the Red Cross, which gave them a sense of participation
in the war effort.[15]

The greatest need that the Red Cross attempted to fill was that of
supplying nurses' aides. The entire nation suffered from a shortage
of nurses; they were drained off by the armed forces, leaving the
civilian population woefully understaffed. Alabama had a shortage

before the war, which only became more severe. The answer was to train volunteers to work a few hours a week under the supervision of registered nurses. The Red Cross, together with the OCD, in both Birmingham and Mobile inaugurated a series of training programs, which consisted of 35 hours of class work and 45 hours of hospital training. The classes were held two hours a day five days a week over a period of seven weeks. Upon completion of the training the women were expected to work 150 hours in a three-month period, which amounted to approximately 2 hours a day. To be eligible for the program, a woman had to be between the ages of eighteen and fifty and a high school graduate. Relatively few Alabama women met these minimum requirements or had the inclination to work outside the home, as shown by the continual recruitment campaigns conducted in the newspapers and the continued shortages in the hospitals. For example, in September 1942 Mobile hospitals had 30 nurses' aides on active duty, but they needed 100 more. In February 1943 Birmingham had 107 trained nurses' aides, but they needed 300 more. By mid-1943 Mobile developed a Junior Nurses' Aide program, which employed the services of juniors and seniors in high school.[16]

Even to persuade women to accept a volunteer job for two hours a day required a change in society's perception of the role of middle-class married women with children. Caring for their families was considered a full-time job and, under normal circumstances, few such women would have considered work outside the home. But these were not normal times, and often women whose husbands were in service volunteered for additional work. Mrs. Sidney Prince of Mobile was typical. Her husband was in the navy and she had two young sons to care for, yet she found time to work as a nurses' aide. Since women of the 1940s viewed a career and marriage as incompatible, Prince was seen as unusual, as witnessed by the description in the headline: "She's a Mother, a Housewife, and a Nurse!" Her eight-year-old son approved of her new role in which she hoped to aid the war effort. By describing her actions, the reporter hoped to persuade other women to follow in her footsteps.[17]

Not only did women have an opportunity to serve as nurses' aides, but they could work for the Red Cross in a number of other capacities. The Production Corps made 90 percent of the surgical dressings that were used by the Army Medical Corps; knitted sweaters, caps, mufflers, helmets, and socks for the soldiers; and made clothes for the war relief program. Five volunteer corps of Jefferson County's Red Cross chapters were assigned duty at the Birmingham Army Air Base, where they sewed, knitted, and made surgical dressings each Wednesday in a room furnished by the hospital. Bessemer women rolled bandages and sewed five days a week from nine to five o'clock at a surgical dressing depot located in the Arlington school. Mobile women turned out two thousand surgical dressings a week for use at the Brookley Field hospital and altered uniforms for the soldiers. Red Cross officials in Mobile had difficulty, however, in staffing their Production Corps after 1943 because those women who were inclined to volunteer offered their services for canteen work, as nurses' aides, aircraft spotters, or for other civilian defense jobs instead. D'Ann Campbell has criticized the Production Corps as a spectacular waste of time.[18] Perhaps the women of Mobile realized that machines could roll bandages better than they could.

Many women worked in the various USO clubs that were established throughout the state. The largest one was in Birmingham, and it provided soldiers with food, entertainment, and a warm welcome to the city. Men came for the weekend from Fort McClellan, Maxwell Field, Craig Field, and Fort Rucker. The first USO Club in Birmingham was small, located on Fourth Avenue North, and it opened immediately after the war began in December 1941. Eventually, the USO acquired use of a large building on Second Avenue North, which had a 450-bed dormitory that was filled every weekend. Approximately forty thousand soldiers used the club's facilities every month. Women whose sons were in the service washed and ironed uniforms and sewed on insignia. They were delighted to do the work because it gave them a chance to talk to the men. Younger women acted as junior hostesses, and they were good talkers, good listeners, and good lookers, according to the soldiers.[19]

Women entertaining soldiers at the Birmingham USO club during the war.
(Courtesy of Archives and Manuscripts, Birmingham Public Library)

One of the services provided by women volunteers at the Birmingham USO
clubs during the war was mending and alteration of servicemen's uniforms.
(Courtesy of Archives and Manuscripts, Birmingham Public Library)

The staff of the Birmingham USO, the director, Bill Bancroft, and Julia R. Walpole, organized the large number of women who acted as hostesses. They received much assistance from local churches and residents of the city. Many families would invite soldiers home for dinner on Sundays. Since meat was rationed, the families had to save their coupons all week so they could serve good dinners to the men. The USO always had more requests for soldiers than there were soldiers available. Walpole described the job as challenging: "You could be sitting and everything so peaceful and quiet, and all of a sudden the door would open and in would march two hundred boys. The commanding officer would announce that they all had to have showers and change their dress and be back at the railroad station within two hours. We managed to do it."[20]

Black women worked in USO clubs which were established for black soldiers. The black USO in Birmingham, organized by the Citizens' Committee for Army Welfare, opened in February 1942 on Fourth Avenue with no money in its budget. This USO was completely separate from the white USO with its own board, director, and junior hostesses. Far fewer activities were available for black soldiers than for white soldiers. The Citizens' Committee also provided the equipment for twenty-three fellowship rooms for the five thousand black soldiers at Fort McClellan. The government made buildings available, but citizens had to supply radios, victrolas, and card tables. Emory O. Jackson, editor of the *Birmingham World,* was the chairman, but black women provided the volunteer services that were necessary to make the USO and the fellowship rooms function. Later other black USO clubs in the state were established in Tuskegee, where the black Army Flying School was located, and in Tuscaloosa.[21]

Although many women took jobs in defense plants or service industries, and others chose to support the war effort by volunteer activities, still others continued their prewar roles as homemakers and mothers. Whatever choice women made, they all had to deal with rationing. The Office of Price Administration began rationing tires in January 1942 and continued rationing items during the entire war. Ration boards were set up in every county in the forty-eight states, and thousands of volunteers were recruited to handle the paperwork involved in controlling prices and issuing a series of ration books to every man, woman, and child in the United States. As the war progressed, nearly every item Americans ate, wore, or used was rationed or regulated. The rationing system was a concentrated attack on wartime inflation and scarcity.

The rationing of gas was announced for the East beginning in May 1942 and was extended nationwide in December, when President Roosevelt ordered a ban on pleasure driving and a thirty-five-mile speed limit on all the nation's highways. The ration system was based on an A, B, and C sticker system. An A sticker owner received the lowest gas allocation, which was four gallons a week. The B and C sticker holders received a supplementary allowance for essential driving or activities. Since motorists were allowed to have only four tires plus a spare, all extra tires over five had to be sold to the government before a ration book could be issued. Motorists devised a wide variety of reasons to convince the OPA that they deserved more gasoline. Those who were not successful were forced to ride streetcars and buses.[22]

Even more important than gasoline rationing was the rationing of food. People managed with less gas by curtailing unnecessary trips and forming car pools, but food rationing hit everyone alike. The OPA issued War Ration Book One in early May 1942. Ration books for each member of a family were distributed at local schools. These books, which were often the first wartime sacrifice required of Americans, contained stamps for items on the ration list such as sugar, coffee, and shoes. Because sugar had been rationed earlier, each housewife had to declare how much sugar she had on hand at home. Equivalent stamps were then torn from the ration book. A wave of buying had begun shortly after Pearl Harbor, and many people had stocked up on sugar and other scarce items. Since twelve ounces of sugar per person per week was not enough for canning, additional sugar was issued for that purpose in August 1942. Neighborhood

HOW MILEAGE IS RATIONED

**The basic ration
for passenger cars**

A ration for holders of passenger car registration cards. Each page of 8 coupons is valid for 2 months.

The gallon value of the coupons is fixed by the Office of Price Administration.

The A ration is designed to provide an average of 240 miles per month; of this 150 miles is for occupational use and 90 miles is for family convenience. This is based on average of 15 miles per gallon.

**Supplemental ration
for passenger cars**

An extra ration for those who must drive more than 150 miles a month for occupational purposes. This ration allows a maximum of 470 miles a month for such purposes.

Holders of B books must carry 3 or more passengers or prove that they cannot, and that other transportation is inadequate.

B drivers receive A and B rations. The B book contains 16 coupons and is valid for 3 to 12 months depending on proven needs.

**Supplemental ration
for essential
passenger cars**

An extra ration for special classes of drivers whose work is most essential to the war effort and who must use their cars more than 470 miles a month for occupational purposes.

C books are valid for 3 months.

Qualified applicants receive both A and C books, providing them with enough gasoline for proven occupational use.

**The ration
for motorcycles**

A ration for holders of motorcycle registration cards. Coupons are good until July 22, 1943.

The D ration is designed to provide an average of 240 miles per month. 150 miles for occupational use. 90 miles for family convenience.

Supplemental D books are issued for proven needs in the same way as B or C books.

T The transport ration for all commercial vehicles (except motorcycles) and military vehicles They receive a T ration but no A ration

E
R The E and R books provide a ration for use highway equipment and purposes. The E book is for small users the R for large users

---

TO QUALIFY FOR MILEAGE RATIONS, YOU MUST COMPLY WITH TIRE REGULATIONS

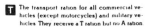

As this chart demonstrates, gasoline rationing was quite restrictive. The basic allotment provided for about 240 miles of driving per month, less than 3,000 miles per year. (December 9, 1942; courtesy of *Birmingham News*)

grocery stores handled these applications. Housewives were allowed to purchase as much sugar as they had used during 1941 for canning.[23]

War Ration Book Two, which was issued in February 1943, had rows of blue and red stamps, marked A, B, C, D, and so on. The blue stamps or points were for processed foods, and the red ones were for meats, cheese, and fats. The previous rationing had been on a single-item basis; one coupon was good for a certain number of pounds of sugar or one pair of shoes. As described by Richard R. Lingeman, "Under the point system, different points values were assigned to different products, enabling the OPA to bring supply more or less in line with demand by making scarce items more expensive in points and lowering the point value of goods that were plentiful." Each man, woman, and child had forty-eight blue points to spend a month, which would buy twenty to twenty-five pounds of canned vegetables a year. Fresh fruits and vegetables were un-rationed. Each person was allotted twenty-eight ounces of meat a week, plus four ounces of cheese. This figure was slightly less than the prewar per capita consumption of two and a half pounds per week.[24]

Women naturally played a large role in implementing this second and challenging rationing system. They were needed to conduct the registration and also to explain the point system to housewives. Mrs. George L. Bailes, director of Jefferson County's Citizens' Service Corps, sent out a call for volunteers for "the biggest job ever under-taken by our government—the issuance of a food ration book for every citizen." An unusually large number of volunteers were needed because it took at least fifteen minutes to explain the system to each applicant. Women were also needed to be on hand at grocery stores the week following the issuance of the books to offer further explanations to shoppers. They were encouraged to volunteer their services to their local grocers. Black women were willing to aid in explaining the rationing program to black consumers, but there is no indication that they were ever allowed to do so. In Birmingham, registration was conducted at the Municipal Auditorium and the local schools during February 22–27, 1943.[25] The Citizens' Service

Corps established a Victory Speakers Bureau, which was prepared to discuss the point system and the second ration book. A third ration book was issued in June 1943, followed by a fourth in October of that year.

An editorial writer for the *Birmingham News* joined Bailes in calling for women volunteers. He felt that it was women's patriotic duty to respond and that their reward would be the knowledge that they were "doing their bit in this emergency." The director of the Jefferson County Rationing Board, J. Frank Ruston, supported the use of volunteers for such jobs, but for a different reason. He said that it was better for both the present and the future of the nation if as many wartime activities as possible were done with cooperative and volunteer help rather than with a paid staff. A large staff of employed personnel would tend to lead the country toward socialism. Volunteer workers would be glad to give up their war activities when peace permitted, but paid workers would want to continue.[26]

The OPA had been divided over the issue of using paid or volunteer workers. The decision was made to use volunteers, the great majority of whom were women. Ruston's comments point to the postwar problem that many Americans were beginning to anticipate: What would be the role of women after their expanded wartime opportunities were gone? Would the traditional gender division of the labor force be altered? In short, would women be willing to return to the kitchen? Ruston clearly realized that if women did only volunteer work, they would have little choice. He also equated working women with socialism.

Volunteer women were also used to enforce the OPA regulations. When the OPA issued an across-the-board consumer price freeze in April 1942, it set up watchdog panels, composed of women, to ensure that the country's two million retailers followed the rules. The women of Mobile and Birmingham, as well as other cities, surveyed the prices in retail stores to determine if they were in line with OPA price ceilings. If any prices were higher than the ceiling, the checker was to notify the owner and request that the price be changed. The price panels proved ineffective save for help in explaining the complexities of the system to neighborhood grocers and shopkeepers. But even when the OPA believed it had evidence of wrongdoing, it rarely took the time or trouble to prosecute businessmen, relying instead on the social stigma attached to buying and selling in the black market.

At the time the fourth ration book was issued in October 1943, housewives were asked to sign a pledge against the black market and inflation. The pledge read: "I will pay no more than top legal prices. I will accept no rationed goods without giving up ration stamps." Every signer of the pledge was expected to support the OPA by checking her shopping list against current ceiling prices and refusing to patronize ration-free black markets. After the pledge was signed, each woman received a window sticker as a symbol of cooperation. Pictures of women whose sons or husbands were in the armed forces were publicized to encourage other women to sign the pledge.[27]

The major purpose of volunteer work in Alabama, as well as nationwide, was to raise the morale of the home front, to demonstrate that all citizens were doing their share, and to bring home to everyone that the nation was involved in a total war. The British and the Russians hardly needed to be reminded that their survival depended on winning the war. To most Alabamians, however, the fighting was far away, and they felt little immediate danger. Not everyone had a relative in the armed forces. Propaganda campaigns alone had little effect, but tying the war to local communities by using residents as airplane spotters, Red Cross workers, nurses' aides, and CSC volunteers made the women feel that they were part of the war effort. Volunteer work encouraged the Alabama public to adopt the values of sacrifice, self-denial, and cooperation, which the government believed were needed to win the war.

CHAPTER 6

Housewives

during Wartime

The work of the housewife has seldom been viewed as important by anyone, including housewives themselves. When asked what they did during the war, countless women replied, "Oh, I was just a housewife." Housework is essential to family life and the economy, but it has often been unnoticed, unrecorded, and unappreciated. The conditions of war made the usual tasks of homemaking—buying, cooking, nursing, consuming, washing, cleaning, and childrearing—more difficult. In addition, the war brought new problems of housing shortages, insufficient schools in areas of increased population, and inadequate medical facilities. These problems were especially critical in Mobile, but they also affected women in Birmingham, Childersburg, Gadsden, and Huntsville. The war subjected women to emotional stress because of the disruption of families, the uncertainties and fears with loved ones in the armed forces, and the shifting employment patterns of husbands. Women coped with all of these problems as they have always done; they met the challenge of maintaining family life during these difficult years.[1]

Nationwide housewives were urged to "use it up, wear it out, make it do, or do without." Women were viewed as soldiers and their "kitchen a combination frontline bunker and rear-echelon miniature war plant." They saved fats and took them to their butcher, where they were exchanged for red points. They were encouraged to save their tin cans by washing the labels off, removing both ends, inserting the extracted tops and bottoms into the cans, and flattening them with their feet. One pound of fat, women were told, contained enough "glycerin to make a pound of black powder—enough for six 75-mm shells or fifty 30-caliber bullets." If every family would save one can a week, this would save "2,500 tons of tin and 190,000 tons of steel—the equivalent of 5,000 tanks or 38 liberty ships."[2] Both black and white Alabama housewives were told, "Turn in your Kitchen Fat—it's worth two Red-Ration Points." An article headlined "From Frying Pan to Firing Line" offered a detailed description of how waste fats were used to manufacture nitroglycerin, dynamite, and gunpowder.[3]

The many service industries devoted to lightening the housewife's load were cut off by the war. Laundry and dry-cleaning establishments were understaffed and their service was slow. The tire shortage and gasoline rationing brought an end to store deliveries. Customers were urged to carry all small packages. Installment buying was drastically limited. Milk deliveries were made every other day. The domestic servant and the once-a-week cleaning woman virtually disappeared from middle- and upper-class homes because of the availability of jobs for women that paid more and offered greater independence.[4]

The lives of many white women in Alabama were affected by the loss or possible loss of black domestic help. Because black help was paid so little, a high proportion of white women had household help. Indeed, more than half of all employed black women worked as domestics in 1940. Some white women were opposed to black women working in war industries because their absence would create an "acute servant problem." Emory O. Jackson believed that this fear explained the widely circulated and baseless rumor that black women were organizing themselves into "Eleanor Clubs" for the purpose of leaving domestic work. These rumors were rampant throughout the South during the war, but no evidence was ever found that such clubs existed. Black women who sought wartime jobs were not attempting to force all black women out of domestic employment but to obtain higher-paying jobs. Black workers could not be expected to remain loyal to their low-paying domestic jobs when service or defense industry jobs at higher wages were available. Jackson opposed what he saw as an attempt to " 'freeze Negro Servants' into jobs which made no contributions to the war effort."[5]

Black women faced discrimination not only from white men but also from white women. A major stumbling block to better race relations had always been antagonism between white and black women, the roots of which were buried in slavery. An expanded role for black women threatened the traditional mistress/maid role that governed relations between white and black women.[6]

Housewives found feeding their families further complicated by the rationing system established by the government in February 1943. Rationing involved a constantly changing system of point values, which was reported in the newspapers. While shopping, the housewife had to keep one eye on the monetary price and the other on the point price. She had to practice double budgeting involving both money and points. She had to keep track of which stamps were valid during a certain period, which were outdated, and what they might buy. The state's newspapers serving both blacks and whites provided a running commentary. The *Birmingham News*, for example, ran a regular column, "Ration Diary, Dates with Uncle Sam":

> May 31—Sugar stamp 12 expires. Coffee stamp becomes good.
> Deadline for tire inspection of C book holders. Red E, F, G expire.
> June 1—Sugar stamp 13 becomes good.
> June 1–10—Return application forms for War Ration Book 3 to OPA
>   Mailing Center, Birmingham.
> June 15—Shoe stamp 17 expires.
> June 16—Shoe stamp 18 becomes good.[7]

Black women encountered problems with regard to the rationing system which white women did not have. Black women did not always have control of their own ration books because government regulations permitted employers to receive War Ration Book Two for their domestic help. Employers would retain the stamps of do-

mestic workers when they ate meals while at work and then sometimes feed them unrationed foods. Black women who worked for
several families had the difficult problem of deciding how to allot
stamps among several employers and still have enough stamps left
over to feed their own families. When black women purchased
rationed foods, merchants in stores would insist on handling their
stamps. Blacks were never sure they retained their fair share of the
ration stamps. The OPA did attempt to make the rules clear to black
women by holding a special session at the Birmingham YMCA to
explain the point system.[8]

Before the rationing program went into effect, housewives and
others often stocked up on items that were in short supply and
thereby actually created shortages. Hoarding was an evil which the
government opposed but never precisely defined. Housewives were
expected to declare their supply of sugar and their stock of canned
goods before they could receive their ration books. Hence the new
rationing ethos made traditional homemaking virtues of planning
ahead obsolete. A newspaper attempted to ridicule hoarding with a
column entitled "Hints for Hoarders" and the following tongue-in-
cheek advice: "Your stocks, piled can on top of can, must truly be a
satisfying sight, one you'd be proud to show the next-door neighbor
or a soldier home from Guadalcanal or a visitor from England. But
just be sure to watch these few things: Turn your cans over often
. . . cans kept for any length of time . . . will swell and finally burst.
And don't store them behind the furnace. . . . They are likely to
spoil!"[9]

Many editorial writers were critical of buying sprees and laid the
blame on women, who did most of the shopping. Women were
accused of storming department stores to buy silk stockings and
shoes, then moving on to grocery stores to buy sugar, coffee, and
milk. The writer viewed such actions as a national disgrace and
encouraged women to ostracize their sisters who hoarded. Many
jokes circulated about the practice of hoarding, indicating a need for
guilty laughter. One concerned a first grader, who listened intently
while the teacher explained the need to save, and replied, "My

mother's saving! She's been saving coffee a long time and now she has a hundred pounds." Another story concerned a man who went to the attic to store his hoard and in the darkness tripped over a big lump—a bag of sugar he had stored during World War I.[10]

Even after housewives had mastered the bureaucratic maze of the rationing system, they had difficulty finding food to buy. Many women had more coupons than storekeepers had meat or canned goods. Shortages developed throughout the state, but the area that was most severely hit was Mobile. The 75 percent increase in population made providing food for that city extremely difficult. By November 1942 grocers' shelves and meat counters lacked the usual supplies, and housewives had difficulty finding adequate food for their families. The basic problem was that the quota of food allotted to Mobile by the OPA was based on its prewar population, not on its greatly expanded numbers. By January 1943 the food shortages coupled with labor problems had closed twenty-five grocery stores. Meat, milk, vegetables, and lard were the items in shortest supply. A. F. Delchamps of the Delchamps Grocery Stores pointed out that rural residents from the surrounding counties, who used to grow their own food and offer some for sale, were now working in war jobs. Up to a thousand additional gallons of milk a day were brought into Mobile from Montgomery, but the milk shortage remained acute. The shortage of fresh milk increased the use of canned milk, and as a result the supply of canned milk decreased. Several dealers reported that they delivered canned milk only with a doctor's prescription.[11]

The Woman's Club of Mobile joined in the campaign to persuade the OPA to revise its methods of establishing quotas for consumer commodities in this defense-crowded area. In November 1943 the OPA announced a new regulation that would provide Mobile with a more equitable food supply. But it was not until the special census of 1944, when the OPA had an actual count of the Mobile population, that the city began to receive its share of consumer commodities.[12]

Shortages of food and rationing encouraged both black and white women to be inventive in planning their menus. They substituted fish, macaroni, noodles, and whole wheat bread for steak, chops, and cutlets. Women's magazines and the women's section of the newspapers were full of new ways to serve nutritional food. Women in Birmingham who attended classes in nutrition were told to consider themselves a "quartermaster corps" geared for the big job of feeding an army of industrial workers. The classes were designed to teach them the science of "eating to win the war." Both rural and urban Alabama women canned, dried, and stored fruits and vegetables for the winter. Pressure cookers were difficult to find, but glass jars and tops were usually available. Working in committees, women throughout the state tried to locate every available canner and sealer so that they could be used as widely as possible. In 1943 the Mobile County Council of Home Demonstration Clubs enrolled 714 women in courses on food conservation. As a result of the program, families produced more year-round gardens and conserved more food for family use.[13]

As homemakers, women in war production areas were especially affected by the shortage of housing. They were faced with making a home out of a tent, a trailer, or even a shack. All areas where defense industries were located experienced housing shortages, but Mobile suffered the greatest dislocations because of the tremendous influx of war workers. At first, workers and their families lived in makeshift shelters. Trailers filled all the available lots and spilled over into new ones. People camped out in tents in cluttered backyards, and some even lived in chicken houses and shelters tacked together out of packing cases. Single men were herded together in boarding- or bunkhouses where they sometimes slept in "hot beds" that were rented for eight-hour shifts.[14] Other workers lived as far away as twenty miles in Foley or even Atmore, compelling them to commute daily.

Blacks in Mobile had even less desirable housing. A survey of black housing made by the YMCA and the women's unit of the USO in July 1942 showed that the needs of black workers were not being met. Fifty black women conducted the survey to determine the living conditions of 20,537 people housed in 3,377 dwellings. All houses were occupied by more people than they were designed to accommodate. For example, 273 two-room dwellings housed 317 families; 213 four-room dwellings housed 585 families. Half of the houses had no electricity; one-fifth had no sewer connections, which meant that one toilet was used by as many as 25 people. The defense housing program overlooked black workers; no clearinghouse existed to aid them in locating housing.[15]

The area surrounding Childersburg, Sylacauga, and Talladega was equally crowded with trailer camps lining the highway in every direction and occupying most of the lots within the communities. Other makeshift arrangements included bunkhouses, tents, camps, and cabins.[16]

In Huntsville workers lived in a government trailer camp that was overcrowded and lacked adequate sanitary facilities. The camp had only one row of outdoor toilets to serve two rows of trailers; water had to be drawn from a well on the sidewalk. Because accommodations for families in the city of Huntsville were almost impossible to find, married men could seldom bring their wives and children with them. They often lived in crowded boardinghouses and were forced to pay for transportation to reach the plant, while supporting a family in another city.[17]

The federal government attempted to meet this housing shortage by the construction of several housing projects. During 1942 some $16 million was invested in Alabama in housing for industrial workers. The largest share went to Mobile, followed by Birmingham. Alabama was second only to Virginia in the numbers and cost of housing for industrial workers. In Mobile, the Federal Housing Authority had constructed sixteen housing projects containing eleven thousand units by the end of the war. Most were located on the outskirts of the city in Prichard, Chickasaw, and Blakely Island. Of the sixteen units, only two were for blacks. The first and most ambitious housing project in Birmingham was the construction in 1942 of three hundred one-story homes on the road leading to the

Municipal Airport near the Chicago Bridge and Iron Company. Housing in this Eastwood area was available only to war workers in Birmingham plants.[18]

Since government construction was not sufficient to relieve the housing shortages in highly congested areas, city officials conducted campaigns in Mobile, Birmingham, and Gadsden to persuade citizens to rent their extra space to war workers. The National Housing Agency surveyed Mobile in August 1943 and determined that living space was available for 6,200 additional people if residents would give up their unused sewing rooms, guest rooms, storage rooms, and studios. A plea was made to rent these 3,440 available rooms before new construction was considered. The next month the Junior Chamber of Commerce, the Mobile War Housing Committee, and the War Housing Center launched a drive to obtain more living quarters for war workers. The slogan was "Share Your Home." The goal of the campaign was to rent all available space and convert properties into additional accommodations by remodeling. Often owners with extra space did not want to rent to families with children. Housing authorities feared war workers would leave if they could not find space for their families. Advertisements in the local newspapers appealed to the patriotism and pocketbooks of residents to rent their extra space.[19] It is impossible to determine the results of this campaign; Mobile probably struggled through the war years with inadequate housing.

In Birmingham with the construction of the Bechtel-McCone-Parsons modification plant in the early months of 1943, an additional three hundred homes were needed. Since all the available rental property was occupied and new construction was at a standstill, a plea went out to private homeowners to split residences into apartments or to open basement servant rooms to homeless workers. The U.S. Employment Service attempted to find local workers for the Bechtel plant because housing for newcomers was virtually nonexistent. Housing remained tight during the war, but Birmingham escaped the chaos of tents, trailers, and shacks that plagued Mobile.[20]

Share Your Home—Rent Your Spare Space For Extra Income!

This is a direct appeal to your patriotism—and an opportunity that means extra money for you, too!

Our city's record war production volume is seriously endangered by an acute housing shortage. Many men and their families who came here to work in our war industries cannot find any home or are trying to live under unbearable conditions.

Your Government is depending on private enterprise as well as public funds to carry out its vast war housing program.

But enough NEW housing simply cannot be built to meet our needs. For construction takes materials needed for ships, planes, tanks and guns.

Property owners and tenants in this city and neighboring communities must answer this problem. If you have vacant space of any kind—spare rooms in your home—space in your attic or over your garage—it can be put to vital use and earn extra money for you. Give vital war workers first chance by phoning the War Housing Center today!

War workers and their families in this city are desperate for lack of living quarters. Unable to obtain housing, they will give up their important war jobs. More must be recruited, but will not come here unless assured of proper housing for their families. Won't you help them—and your country—and earn extra income besides?

Mobile residents were encouraged to rent out extra space in their homes to help alleviate the housing shortage. (*Mobile Register,* October 12, 1943; courtesy of University of South Alabama Library)

The industrial city of Gadsden also experienced severe housing shortages. With increased numbers of workers, housing was tight and rooms and hotel rooms were at a premium. Many homeowners added a room or apartment to their present structures to accommodate war workers. It was estimated that there were 2,270 more families than housing units in 1943. The housing situation was acute, but Gadsden did not resort to tents and trailers as other towns had because the prewar labor surplus meant that fewer newcomers were attracted to the city.[21]

The public schools of the state were overcrowded and understaffed during the war. Mothers would often find their children being forced to attend split sessions or even, as in the case of Mobile, with no classes to attend. In such situations, women had to instruct their children as best they could at home. For its size, the Childersburg school saw the greatest increase in student enrollment; in one year the student body nearly doubled. In 1940–41 the school had an enrollment of 470 and employed 13 teachers; the following year the student population increased to 900 with each teacher assigned between 70 and 80 students.[22]

The schools for black children had always been inferior to those for white children, but the gulf widened during the war years. As early as 1942 epidemics and disease spread throughout the twenty-four black schools in Birmingham. Classes were more crowded than usual with East Birmingham, for example, having 226 students and only three teachers. Schools lacked adequate toilets, drinking fountains, and cloakrooms. Black mothers were urged to learn about the nutrition program at the schools, such as the school lunch program, the Food Stamp plan, and the Penny Milk program. They were encouraged to ask, "Are the colored kids in your town getting their share of these benefits?"[23]

The Mobile city school system was overwhelmed by the children of the new labor force. The problem became acute as early as September 1942. By this time the population had increased by 50 percent, and the school system, which had been inadequate before the war, was unable to provide classes for all the children. During the school year 1942–43, double shifts of four hours each were conducted, but even then two thousand white students had no classes to attend. No one knew how many black children were not attending schools, but the proportion was probably higher. The superintendent and the school board looked to the federal government for assistance and were slow to make plans of their own.

The leadership of the school system came under fire both from Agnes Meyer, a *Washington Post* writer who traveled through the South in 1943 investigating war towns, and from the editors of the *Mobile Register.* Meyer described the superintendent as a man of seventy-four who offered inadequate leadership and should have retired years earlier. The Mobile editor criticized the superintendent and the board for being slow in resolving the school crisis of 1942–43. The school year 1943–44 was about to begin, and little had been done to alleviate the problems. Finally, plans were laid to build a forty-room school in Prichard, a twenty-eight room school on South Ann Street, and a sixteen-room school on Blakely Island, but only after much pressure had been applied by the Chamber of Commerce, the War Manpower Commission, and editorials in the *Register*. The city leaders feared that war workers with children would leave the area and wartime production of ships would decrease. Mobile struggled through another academic year because these new schools did not open until March 1944.[24]

In addition to a shortage of classrooms, Mobile developed a teacher shortage. Salaries of teachers were low, compared not only with national but also with regional averages. A National Education Association survey in 1940–41 of thirteen southern cities placed Mobile salaries in twelfth place for elementary teachers and eleventh place for high school teachers. In the elementary grades, a white teacher with two years of college received $800 a year; those who had completed three years earned $850; and college graduates started at $950. The maximum they might hope to earn was $1,300. White high school teachers began with $1,150; after long years of service, women might receive $1,700 and men $2,100. The salaries for blacks were even lower. Many teachers left these low-paying jobs for war work because a typist could make $1,440 and a shipyard worker nearly $3,000.[25]

Not only did Alabama mothers sometimes have to teach their children, but occasionally they also had to be doctor and nurse. The war created shortages of medical services nationwide because 50,000 of the country's approximately 185,000 doctors were in the armed forces. Alabama was especially affected because in 1943 the state had one doctor for every 2,671 people, whereas the recommended safe minimum was one doctor for every 1,500 people.[26]

Mobile experienced the most severe medical crisis in the state during the war. In addition to a shortage of doctors and hospital facilities, an epidemic of flu and meningitis struck the city. Most of the meningitis victims were children whose mothers were forced to care for them at home because the hospital did not have an isolation ward. It was only after a public outcry and much pressure from the newspapers that an isolation ward was created.

During the winter of 1942–43, Mobile escaped serious epidemics despite the shortage of medical services. Officials of the Mobile Health Department assumed that the city would be equally fortunate the following winter. One department official spoke to the teachers at the opening of the school term in September 1943 and discounted fears of epidemics. He felt disease could be combated by teachers emphasizing good health instruction, encouraging immunization against diphtheria, smallpox, and whooping cough, and maintaining the sanitary equipment of the schools. But in January 1944 the number of cases of influenza increased to two thousand and health officers warned Mobilians to consider the illness seriously and take necessary precautions. Eventually half of the population was affected to some extent by this virus.[27]

In February 1944, a much more serious crisis developed with an outbreak of meningitis. During this crisis, several people died because they were denied treatment at the city hospitals. The hospitals would not admit and treat meningitis patients because they had no isolation wards. Fearing the danger of communicating the disease to others in the hospital, officials sent patients back to their homes, boardinghouses, or rooms to wait out the course of the disease. Two eighteen-year-old women died in February 1944, one twenty-four hours after she was turned away from the hospital and the other on a visit home from college. A little girl with diphtheria was treated in the emergency room, then sent back home, where she subsequently died. Another family drove forty miles in the rain with a baby who had spinal meningitis, only to be turned away.[28]

The local newspapers publicized the situation and attacked the do-nothing policy in editorials. One editorial was entitled "Let's Quit Playing the Role of an Ostrich!" Another said: "That such a situation should exist in a metropolitan city in the year 1944 is well-nigh barbaric in its implications. In the Stone Age primitive men drove their fellow tribesmen into the forest to die when they contracted leprosy and other communicable diseases. Mobile's methods of dealing with communicable diseases is not so much more merciful than that pursued by the men of the Stone Age."[29]

By February 1944 the city was averaging a case a day, and that rate was expected to continue until spring. Finally, the Mobile Board of Health passed a resolution recommending that a portion of the City Hospital be set aside as an isolation ward. The City Commission and the County Board of Revenue agreed to provide the necessary funds to operate the section. The Sisters of Mercy, who operated the hospital, reached an agreement with the city and work was begun on the long overdue wing, which finally opened on March 5. This decision was good news to mothers who had been caring for their sick children at home. For example, twelve-year-old Jerry Crutchfield became ill while he was at school; he went to the hospital, where a spinal test showed he had meningitis, but was sent home to recover from the disease as best he could. His mother had to care for him until the new ward opened.[30]

For the majority of Alabama housewives, living in wartime was more complicated than in peacetime. Despite the highest family income in more than a decade, most housewives found it difficult to care for their families; they were not able to use the extra cash to lighten their work load. Buying and preparing food took more time and effort because of the shortages and rationing. Congested living conditions in the boom areas made adequate housing almost impossible to find. Women tried to make a warm home life in flimsy trailers, crowded apartments, and overpriced houses. Mothers had to deal with half-day school sessions for their children in crowded classrooms. They were forced to cope with shortages of doctors and inadequate hospital facilities. They stood in long lines for countless purposes. But through it all they devised ways to keep their families clothed, healthy, and well fed. In short, they successfully met the challenge of maintaining family life in wartime.

Conclusion

The war years brought about great changes in the society and economy of Alabama. The shortage of men and the demand for goods and services provided women with an opportunity to expand their role in the workplace and in volunteer activities. These changes affected different women in different ways; some were beneficial, others detrimental. The experience of a welder, an airplane mechanic, a Red Cross worker, or a textile worker was different from that of a black woman who left field work for a job in a laundry. The most visible change of the war was the imperative need for women workers. Along with wider job opportunities went higher wages, less discrimination, greater recognition of the value of women as workers, and concern for women's dual responsibilities as mothers and workers.

Nationwide the war economy brought about substantial changes in the size of the female labor force and the characteristics of the women who worked. The first of these changes was a tremendous increase in the number of women who were employed. Nationally the female labor force grew by 6.5 million from 1940 to 1945; the proportion of employed women to the total female population jumped from 25 to 36 percent. The second big change was the composition of the female labor force, which shifted to include large numbers of married and older women. One in every ten married women took a job during the war. For the first time in the nation's history, more married women than single women were in the work force. Women with children also represented a significant proportion of the wartime increase in female employment. Older women, too, made a major contribution to the war economy as more than two million women over the age of thirty-five entered the work force. According to Hartmann, "The typical female worker had changed from one who was young and single to one who was older and married."[1]

Since slightly more than half of all Alabama women were employed in Mobile, measuring their experience with that of women nationally can provide a useful comparison. One of the first facts to emerge is that female employment in Mobile showed marked differences from that in the nation as a whole. More Mobile women worked before the war than nationwide, and the wartime increase was smaller. In 1940, 31 percent of Mobile women were employed, an unusually high figure; but by 1944 it had increased to only 35 percent.[2] The major reason for these differences is almost certainly the presence of a large number of black women in the Mobile labor force. Since black women have always worked in larger numbers than white women, a meaningful picture can be obtained only by separating the figures for black and white women. These two groups experienced the war in very different ways.

The first big difference between the two groups is that white women moved into Mobile in far greater numbers than did black women. Of the migrants into the area, 85 percent were white and only 15 percent were black. Hence the white female population increased nearly three times during the war, but the black female population increased by less than one-fourth. These figures indicate that white women were able to recognize the economic opportunity and were in a position to take advantage of wartime employment in far greater numbers than blacks.[3]

The employment of white women in Mobile closely parallels that of all women nationwide. The proportion of white women who were employed in Mobile rose from 27 percent in 1940 to 37 percent in

1944, which is very near the national increase. Employed white Mobile women also tended to be older and married, as were women nationally. In 1940 only 21 percent of Mobile's white women over the age of twenty-five were employed, but by 1944 the figure had risen to 32 percent. Before the war only 16 percent of Mobile's married white women over twenty-five were employed; that figure rose to 20 percent by the war's end.[4]

Black women had a different experience. Because they had always been employed in greater numbers, black women were less affected by the war than were white women. In fact, black women's share of the Mobile labor force declined from 54 percent in 1940 to 46 percent in 1944. This decline was attributable to the tremendous increase in the number of employed white women; in absolute numbers black women show a slight increase, but it was dwarfed by the large number of whites. The decline of black women's share of the labor force was even greater with regard to married women. In 1940 half of all Mobile black married women worked, but in 1944 this number had dropped to 40 percent. This decline may have been caused by increased economic opportunities for their husbands. Black women between the ages of eighteen and twenty-four profited the most from the wartime economy. The number employed in that age group more than doubled, whereas that in all other age categories remained constant.[5]

These figures illustrate the different experiences of white and black women. White women worked only when they were young, and even those tended to drop out of the job market after they married. The norm for white women was to remain at home as wives and mothers; the great majority could do so because their husbands or someone else supported them. Black women did not have this option. They had to work either to support themselves or somebody else; more than half of all black women worked all their lives.

The type of work that women in Mobile did and the numbers involved changed drastically. Spectacular increases occurred in manufacturing. In 1940 only 1,300 women were employed in this field, but by 1944 the number had increased more than five times to 6,700. An even greater increased occurred among those who worked for the federal government. Before the war only 200 women held such jobs, but that number increased to 7,200 by 1944. (These women were employed at Brookley Field, which did not exist before 1940.) Those employed in trades and services increased much less, although even here the number more than doubled from 5,300 to 11,500.[6] Hence Mobile women had more opportunities for employment than were available in other parts of the state.

Again the experience of white and black women was different. Evidence indicates that white women were able to obtain the overwhelming majority of the manufacturing and government jobs. For the first time white women worked at men's jobs and earned men's wages. Before the war white women worked in laundries, restaurants, hotels, and retail and wholesale trade. These are all fields characterized by low pay and poor working conditions. During the war white women were able to find employment in aircraft maintenance, shipbuilding, and ordnance depots. These jobs represented a significant step up the occupational ladder because wages were higher than in traditional female occupations. Black women also experienced some mobility; they moved from agriculture and domestic work to the trade and service jobs that the white women had vacated. This can be viewed as a step up, but because of the intense racism in the state, black women remained in the same relative position in the labor market.[7]

But along with these changes in the female work force were factors that limited women's goals and options. The new economic opportunities were based on a temporary wartime need. The invitations to women to step outside their customary sphere were offered in terms that reinforced traditional ideas about sex roles. Government propaganda appealed to women's patriotism and obligation to their nation rather than to personal satisfaction or financial need, thus reinforcing the temporary nature of their duty. Propaganda further highlighted women's femininity and continued to view women in relation to men. Mothers constantly heard about the undesirable effects their employment might have on their children. With this approach, the public could accept the participation of women in unusual roles without surrendering basic beliefs about those roles.

The major recruiting theme of defense industries was an appeal to patriotism. Women were urged to fulfill their duty as citizens to hasten the day of victory. They could save lives by taking jobs and thus help win the war sooner. Women were never encouraged to seek work for the income it would bring. For example, the women welders in Mobile were portrayed as stepping in to take the place of men in the vital war industries, not as needing to work for a living. Likewise, the women who worked in the Huntsville Arsenal were said to believe that the money side of the job was secondary. Women were never encouraged to work for personal satisfaction. Their satisfaction was to come from their support of the nation in wartime. This appeal to patriotism made the work temporary because at the war's end this motivation would no longer be valid.

Care was always taken to preserve the image of women's femininity. Pictures of women welders with their helmets pushed back applying lipstick assured readers that these workers were still women underneath their heavy welding clothes. A Brookley Field newsletter carried pictures showing the same women workers in their working clothes and in formal dress, confirming the view that airplane mechanics were also beautiful women. The women's counselor at ADDSCO confirmed women's continued interest in feminine topics by indicating that she discussed recipes, babies, and hairdos with the women workers. As long as women were still feminine, no change had occurred in sex roles.

At the same time that the public was being assured that women were still the weaker, passive sex, other observers noted that these women were performing superhuman tasks. The workers in the Huntsville Arsenal were described as "modern Amazons" from Madison County, who were performing their work in an amazing fashion. One worker was able to "do anything on the line that any man can do." She was "a slim girl, weighing merely 105 pounds but 'can take it,' as the foreman commented, better than any man he ever saw." Women welders in Mobile were described as "doing jobs of men, doing them as well, sometimes better" than men.[8] Such statements led people to fear that women would become too strong, that they would dress like men, talk like men, and develop powerful biceps. This excessively lavish praise indicated a certain uneasiness about women assuming these new roles.

The greatest burden laid on women was that their children would suffer if they worked outside the home. Those who criticized working women, such as Bishop Toolen, questioned whether the war would be won on foreign battlefields and lost at home. The general attitude was that the welfare of children and the future of the nation rested upon mothers: "To insist that these mothers are more essential to war industries than to their children and to deny children their mother's care, results in child neglect, juvenile delinquency, and the undermining of national security."[9] This point of view assumed that women did not really need to work and that they had a choice in the matter. Yet the great majority of women who worked did so because they had to support themselves or others.

Hence many forces operated upon women to keep them in their proper sphere, despite the new roles they were asked to play during the war. The fear that women's wartime experiences threatened the traditional sex-gender system was evident in the media, in which a variety of authorities sought to restrict women's public activities. At the beginning of the war, Alabamians appeared to support the government in its drive to recruit women, as evidenced by the great concern with establishing day care centers. But this support was short-lived. By mid-1943, social workers, the press, and the public shifted their concern to what they saw as the rising tide of juvenile delinquency that was threatening the American home. Social welfare and child care experts called upon women to pay more attention to their maternal duties. From this time on, working women encountered greater resistance from the public. By the end of the war, businessmen and government officials were telling women to relinquish their jobs to veterans and return to the kitchen. Despite their wishes, women were forced to return to lower-paying jobs.

The state legislature had an opportunity to reevaluate women's legal status in February 1945, when a group of women requested the right to serve on juries. Women leaders, recognizing that the war had the potential to bring changes in women's roles, began as early as June 1942 to build support for female jury service. A group of women appeared before the state legislature in 1943 and argued that with the shortage of manpower, women should be allowed to serve on juries. Ida Rosenthal, an attorney from Birmingham, said, "Women can do anything men can do—they are doing things that men do in the war—and women are able to take care of themselves." Mrs. J. Bruce Airey, a prominent clubwoman from Wetumpka, pointed out that twenty-six states, including Louisiana and Kentucky, allowed women to serve on juries and Alabama should follow in their footsteps. Despite the arguments of women, in February 1945 a House committee rejected the proposal by a vote of 6 to 3.[10] This decision indicates that state legislators did not believe that women's participation in the work force warranted a change in their legal position.

In the years immediately following the end of the war, female employment in the state drastically declined. Bechtel-McCone-Parsons and Brookley Field cut back as the need for airplane modification, repair, and maintenance almost vanished; ADDSCO, the Gulf Shipbuilding Company, Alabama Ordnance Depot, and Redstone and Huntsville Arsenals no longer had large wartime contracts. White working-class women lost their high-paying jobs and were forced to seek other work. Black women lost their service jobs and had to return to domestic service. Women's net gains during the war years were almost negligible. By 1950 statewide female employment was only slightly higher than it had been in 1940. Before the war began, 24 percent of all women in the state were employed; by 1950 the percent had increased to only 26, which was below the national average of 29 percent.[11]

These figures suggest that the war did not bring about long-term changes in the position of women statewide. Once again, however, we need to separate the employment figures for black and white women to gain a clearer picture. White women throughout the state experienced a phenomenal growth in employment; their labor force participation rate increased from 17 percent in 1940 to 23 percent in 1950. This 6 percentage point increase is even more impressive when compared with the previous decade, during which white women's employment saw virtually no increase. White women did not retain their high-paying war jobs, but they saw substantial growth in clerical and sales jobs. In 1940 only 29 percent of white women held such jobs, but by 1950 the proportion had increased to 39 percent. The percentages of professional and operative women workers, however, suffered a slight decline.[12]

The experience of black women was quite different. Their share of employment actually declined from 36 percent in 1940 to 34 percent in 1950. Their representation in the labor force also declined in absolute numbers. Like white women, black women were not able to hold on to wartime gains. Once again, they were forced to take jobs as domestics and farm workers, although in somewhat smaller numbers. The percent of blacks who were employed as domestics decreased from 53 in 1940 to 46 in 1950; that of farm workers declined from 17 percent to 10 percent. Black women were able to retain some wartime service jobs. The percent of service jobs doubled from 7 to 15 percent.[13]

World War II had some positive effects on white women, but it had less effect on the condition of black women. Employment of white women greatly increased relative to prewar times, but it still remained well below the national average. Alabama women did not work in as large numbers as women nationwide either before or after the war. White Alabama women enjoyed a few brief years of good pay, but most of the gains were eroded at the end of the war. The expanding economy of the postwar years did allow most white women who wanted work to find it, but at reduced wages. Their unemployment rate in the state dropped from 15 percent in 1940 to almost 4 percent by 1950. Black women saw fewer gains. They had found better jobs in service industries for a brief period, then they were forced back into domestic work at the war's end. Because of the racial attitudes in the state, Alabama black women had not achieved the inroads into white-collar or manufacturing jobs that they did nationwide. But they too were able to find more jobs in a growing postwar economy. The black unemployment rate declined from 9 percent in 1940 to 5 percent in 1950.[14]

Does all this indicate a turning point in the lives of Alabama women? Did it permanently alter their relation to wage work? The evidence offers little to those who suggest that such was the case. Employment of women did increase, but this trend had been under way at least since 1920 and would probably have continued even without a war. The general pattern of women's employment remained much the same as before the war. Women worked at the same jobs both before and after the war. Hence the boom of the war years is best understood as a temporary response to a national emergency rather than a breakthrough in new economic opportunities for women.

This is not to say, however, that some doors were not opened. Some women became aware of possibilities they had not previously considered. World War II did promote changes in the lives of individual women. According to Elizabeth Sisson, the war brought a "tremendous change" in her life. She had married immediately after high school and had a baby "because there was nothing else to do" during the Depression. The war started shortly after her baby was born, and she moved from Birmingham to Mobile, where she took a job at Brookley Field. She had found housework boring, but she loved working at Brookley: "It was exciting for me to get dressed to go to work every morning, to be with people."[15]

Mayme Kirby, who was a widow with two children to support, described the war years as "the time that the doors were really open to women to work most anywhere they really wanted to." Mary Stinson said, "World War II brought about the change really, in women's working habits. . . . This was the beginning of a new era for women." Young unmarried women, who flocked to Mobile in search of jobs, had the opportunity to live alone or with other women in apartments. Such independent living arrangements away from their parents marked a tremendous change in lifestyle of southern women.[16]

The social workers of the state knew and dealt with women who experienced a new sense of independence with an income of their own for the first time. Women from farm families began to realize that they had earning power. For generations the women in these families had been housekeepers and never thought of jobs outside the home. But with the war came jobs and a new sense of self. Some women became dissatisfied with the humdrum of everyday life; they were discontent and no longer willing to tolerate the unpleasantness at home which they formerly accepted. Husbands in these cases were bewildered and at a loss to understand the changed attitude of their wives. One husband begged a social worker to "make his wife go back home and do right."[17] For these women the war gave employment a patriotic sanction it would not otherwise have had. But the experiences of these women turned out to be ephemeral and failed to add up to significant changes in their status.

World War II ended the Depression and laid the foundation for postwar economic growth. The war expanded job opportunities temporarily for women and added a greater element of choice to their lives. The wartime labor shortage forced employers to hire married women and older women and allowed them to prove their capabilities. But demonstration of effectiveness at tough jobs did not change attitudes about women's work in general or about their primary role as homemakers. White women worked in much larger numbers after the war, but they continued to be employed in the same jobs as before. They were still inclined to regard themselves primarily as wives and mothers and subordinated their work plans to family needs. They viewed their work as a job rather than a career. Opportunities for black women decreased, and even those who were employed were still limited primarily to domestic work. The war provided Alabama women with a brief period during which they assumed unaccustomed roles, but it does not appear to have brought about profound change in their status. The forces of continuity seem to have prevailed over the forces of change during the war years in Alabama.

Notes

Introduction

1. William H. Chafe, *The American Woman: Her Changing Social, Economic, and Political Roles, 1920–1970* (New York: Oxford University Press, 1972), 195.

2. Leila J. Rupp, *Mobilizing Women for War: German and American Propaganda, 1939–1945* (Princeton: Princeton University Press, 1978), 137–66.

3. Karen Anderson, *Wartime Women: Sex Roles, Family Relations, and the Status of Women during World War II* (Westport, Conn.: Greenwood Press, 1981), 154–78.

4. Eleanor Straub, "United States Government Policy toward Civilian Women during World War II," *Prologue* 5 (Winter 1973): 240–54.

5. D'Ann Campbell, *Women at War with America: Private Lives in a Patriotic Era* (Cambridge, Mass.: Harvard University Press, 1984), 220–26.

6. Susan M. Hartmann, *The Home Front and Beyond: American Women in the 1940s* (Boston: G. K. Hall/Twayne, 1982), 209–16.

Chapter 1

1. Rosalyn Baxandall, Linda Gordon, and Susan Reverby, eds., *America's Working Women* (New York: Vintage Books, 1976), 280.

2. Mary P. Ryan, *Womanhood in America* (New York: New Viewpoints, 1975), 188.

3. Susan Hartmann, *The Home Front and Beyond: American Women in the 1940s* (Boston: J. K. Hall/Twayne, 1982), 18.

4 U.S. Department of Commerce, Bureau of the Census, *Sixteenth Census of the United States: 1940,* Vol. 2, *Characteristics of the Population* (Washington D.C.: U.S. Government Printing Office, 1943), 235.

5. Ibid., 233.

6. U.S. Department of Labor, Women's Bureau, Special Bulletin 1, *Effective Industrial Use of Women in the Defense Program* (Washington, D.C.: U.S. Government Printing Office, 1940), 4.

7. Nancy Woloch, *Women and the American Experience* (New York: Alfred A. Knopf, 1984), 461–62.

8. Susan Estabrook Kennedy, *If All We Did Was to Weep at Home: A History of White Working-Class Women in America* (Bloomington: Indiana University Press, 1979), 189–90.

9. "Labor Market Developments Report for Birmingham," June 1, 1943, Records of the Bureau of Employment Security, Record Group 183, Box 1, National Archives (hereafter abbreviated as RG and NA). See also "Labor Market Developments Report for Mobile," June 12, 1943, ibid., Box 3; "Labor Market Developments Report for Talladega," Aug. 8, 1943, ibid., Box 5; "Labor Market Developments Report for Huntsville," Aug. 9, 1943, ibid., Box 3; "Labor Market Developments Report for Anniston," June 12, 1943, ibid., Box 1; "Labor Market Developments Report for Montgomery," June 15, 1943, ibid., Box 3.

10. Chauncey Sparks, "The Impact of the War on Alabama," in *War Comes to Alabama* (University, Ala.: University of Alabama, 1943), 4.

11. *Birmingham News,* Jan. 17, 1943; "Labor Market Developments Report for Birmingham," June 1, 1943.

12. *Birmingham News,* Feb. 14, 1943; "Labor Market Developments Report for Gadsden," Apr. 15, 1943, Bureau of Employment Security, RG 183, Box 2, NA.

13. "Labor Market Developments Report for Anniston," Oct. 15, 1943, Bureau of Employment Security, RG 183, Box 1, NA; "Labor Market Development Report for Decatur," Aug. 11, 1943, ibid., Box 2.

14. Melton McLaurin and Michael Thomason, *Mobile: The Life and Times of a Great Southern City* (Woodland Hills, Calif.: Windsor Publications, 1981), 124.

15. "Survey of the Mobile Employment Stabilization Plan," June 1943, Bureau of Employment Security, RG 183, Box 3, NA.

16. *Birmingham News,* May 23, 1943.

17. *Birmingham News,* Jan. 17, Sept. 3, 4, 1943; Sparks, "Impact of the War on Alabama," 2.

18. George B. Tindall, *The Emergence of the New South, 1913–1945* (Baton Rouge: Louisiana State University Press, 1967), 679–98.

19. *Birmingham News,* Mar. 7, 14, Apr. 25, 1943; Sparks, "Impact of the War on Alabama," 1–2.

20. Sparks, "Impact of the War on Alabama," 2; *Birmingham News,* Mar. 28, May 16, 1943.

21. *Birmingham News,* Feb. 28, Apr. 31, May 23, 1942, Feb. 21, Apr. 18, 1943, Jan. 14, 1944.

22. Tindall, *Emergence of the New South,* 701.

23. Sparks, "Impact of the War on Alabama," 5.

24. "National Defense Migration in the Southeast," *Alabama Social Welfare* (State Department of Public Welfare, Montgomery, Ala.), June 1942. This journal was published monthly by the Alabama Department of Public Welfare and is deposited at the Alabama Department of History and Archives in Montgomery. See also *Birmingham News,* Apr. 8, 1942.

25. U.S. Department of Commerce, Bureau of the Census, *Characteristics of the Population, Labor Force, Families, and Housing, Mobile Congested Production Area,* 1, Mar. 1944, Table I (Washington, D.C.: U.S. Government Printing Office, 1944); Bernadette Kuehn Loftin, "A Social History of the Mid-Gulf South: Panama City–Mobile, 1930–1950" (Ph.D. dissertation, University of Southern Mississippi, 1971), 273–331.

26. The population of Mobile County, as opposed to the metropolitan area, increased 64.7 percent. Comparable figures for the other congested production areas in order of their increase in population were Hampton Roads (44.7 percent), San Diego (43.7 percent), Charleston (38.1 percent), Portland-Vancouver (31.8 percent), San Francisco (25 percent), Puget Sound (20 percent), Los Angeles (15.1 percent), Muskegon, Michigan (14.4 percent), and Detroit–Willow Run (8.2 percent).

27. *Mobile Press,* Sept. 18, 1942. The exact figures are as follows: retail trade up from $33 million to $65 million in two years, wholesale trade $50 million to $100 million, industrial employees 20,000 to 60,000, daily phone calls 100,000 to 300,000, and newspaper circulation 42,000 to 75,000.

28. McLaurin and Thomason, *Mobile,* 127; Loftin, "Social History of the Mid-Gulf South," 289.

29. *Mobile Register,* Sept. 18, 1942.

30. *Birmingham News,* Mar. 10, 1944.

31. *Birmingham News,* Jan. 31, 1943. Virginia Van Der Veer Hamilton is today a professor of history at the University of Alabama at Birmingham.

32. "Survey of the Employment Situation in the Childersburg, Alabama,

Area," Dec. 15, 1941, Bureau of Employment Security, RG 183, Box 2, NA; "Labor Market Developments Report for Talladega," Dec. 10, 1943, Bureau of Employment Security, RG 183, Box 5, NA.

33. "The Powder Mill Town," *Alabama Social Welfare*, June 1942, pp. 5–9; *Birmingham News*, Mar. 7, 14, 1943.

34. "Childersburg in Production," *Alabama Social Welfare*, Aug. 1942, pp. 13–16.

35. "Labor Market Developments Report for Anniston," Apr. 20, 1943, Bureau of Employment Security, RG 183, Box 1, NA; "Office of Community War Services, Report on Anniston, Alabama War Area," Apr. 6, 1944, ibid.; *Birmingham News*, Feb. 21, 1943.

36. "Labor Market Developments Report for Gadsden," Apr. 15, 1943; *Birmingham News*, Feb. 14, 1943.

37. *Huntsville Times*, Oct. 23, 30, Nov. 30, 1941; *Birmingham News*, Apr. 25, 1943; "National Defense Migration in the Southeast," *Alabama Social Welfare*, June 1942, p. 11.

38. National Planning Association, "Committee on Post-War Employment Problems," Report on Huntsville, Ala., Feb. 1943, Committee for Congested Production Areas, RG 212, Box 37, NA.

39. *Montgomery Advertiser*, Jan. 4, 1942, Jan. 14, 1943; *Birmingham News*, Feb. 28, 1943.

Chapter 2

1. Leila Rupp, *Mobilizing Women for War: German and American Propaganda, 1939–1945* (Princeton: Princeton University Press, 1978), 94–95; Office of War Information, Advance Release, Oct. 19, 1942, U.S. Women's Bureau, RG 86, Box 1536, NA; "Basic Program Plan for Womanpower," Aug. 1943, Office of War Information, RG 208, Box 587, NA.

2. *Birmingham News*, July 26, Aug. 23, 1942, Jan. 10, 12, 1943; *Mobile Press Register*, Sept. 13, 20, Nov. 23, 1942.

3. "Resurvey 1 of the Employment Situation in the Mobile Area of Alabama," U.S. Employment Service, Sept. 23, 1942, Bureau of Employment Security, RG 183, Box 3, NA.

4. *Mobile Press Register*, Sept. 13, 1942.

5. Mary Anderson, "Women at Work," Jan. 25, 1942, Women's Bureau, RG 86, Box 1537, NA.

6. "Resurvey 1 of the Employment Situation in the Mobile Area of Alabama," U.S. Employment Service, Sept. 23, 1942.

7. *Mobile Press Register,* Sept. 20, 1942; *Mobile Register,* Nov. 23, 1942.

8. "Labor Market Developments Report for the Mobile Area," Oct. 28, 1942; "Survey Mobile Employment Stabilization Plan," June 1943, "Mobile Demand-Supply Supplement," July 1944, Nov. 1944, all in Bureau of Employment Security, RG 183, Box 3, NA.

9. *Mobile Register,* Sept. 26, 1942; *Mobile Press Register,* Oct. 3, 22, 1943.

10. *Mobile Press Register,* Sept. 26, 1943.

11. "Labor Market Developments Report for Mobile," Oct. 28, 1942, June 12, 1943; "Mobile Demand-Supply Supplement," Nov. 1944, both in Bureau of Employment Security, RG 183, Box 3, NA.

12. *Mobile Press Register,* Feb. 21, 1943; *Mobile Register,* Jan. 23, 1943; Eleanor Straub, "United States Government Policy toward Civilian Women during World War II," *Prologue* 5 (Winter 1973): 240–54.

13. *Mobile Register,* Jan. 23, Feb. 6, 11, 1943.

14. *Mobile Press Register,* Feb. 21, 1943.

15. Ibid.

16. *Mobile Register,* Feb. 23, 1943; *Mobile Press,* Mar. 1, 5, 7, 1943. This statement referred to a plan to conscript women, which was briefly considered by Congress in 1942.

17. *Mobile Register,* Jan. 28, 1943.

18. Rupp, *Mobilizing Women for War,* 138.

19. U.S. Department of Commerce, Bureau of the Census, *Sixteenth Census of the United States: 1940,* Vol. 2, *Characteristics of the Population* (Washington, D.C.: U.S. Government Printing Office, 1943), 235; Rupp, *Mobilizing Women for War,* 141–43; Karen Anderson, *Wartime Women: Sex Roles, Family Relations, and the Status of Women during World War II* (Westport, Conn.: Greenwood Press, 1981), 61–62; U.S. Department of Labor, Women's Bureau, Bulletin 209, *Women Workers in Ten War Production Areas and Their Postwar Employment Plans* (Washington, D.C.: U.S. Government Printing Office, 1946).

20. *Mobile Press Register,* Oct. 11, 1942.

21. Ibid., Sept. 13, 1942.

22. Ibid.

23. Ibid.; *Birmingham News,* July 7, 1943.

24. *Birmingham News,* Feb. 21, 1943; Rupp, *Mobilizing Women for War,* 96.

25. *Mobile Register,* Feb. 6, 1943.

26. Maureen Honey, *Creating Rosie the Riveter: Class, Gender, and*

Propaganda during World War II (Amherst: University of Massachusetts Press, 1984), 19–24.

27. Women's Bureau, *Women Workers in Ten War Production Areas;* Honey, *Creating Rosie the Riveter,* 26–27.

28. *Mobile Press Register,* Apr. 9, June 25, 1944.

29. *Birmingham News,* Sept. 13, 1942.

30. *Mobile Press Register,* Sept. 13, 1942.

31. *Birmingham World,* Mar. 31, 1942; *Birmingham News,* Oct. 18, Dec. 11, 22, 1942; *Mobile Press Register,* Dec. 15, 1942; Engineering, Science, and Management War Training, List of Approved Courses, July 1, 1942, Women's Bureau, RG 86, Box 1543, NA.

32. *Mobile Press Register,* May 16, 1943; "Labor Market Developments Report for Mobile," Jan. 12, 1943, Bureau of Employment Security, RG 183, Box 3, NA.

33. "United States Employment Service, Bulletin 514," Mar. 31, 1943, War Manpower Commission, RG 211, Box 2-703, NA.

34. Final Disposition Report, Case No. 7-GR-141 and 7-GR-125, Box 753, FEPC Records, RG 228, Atlanta Branch, NA; *Birmingham World,* July 13, 1943.

Chapter 3

1. "Mobile Demand-Supply Supplement for the Mobile Labor Market Area," Mar. 1944, Bureau of Employment Security, RG 183, Box 3, NA.

2. *Brookley Bay Breeze,* May 3, 1943; *A la Moad,* Oct. 18, 1943. These newsletters, published by MoASC during the war, are deposited at the Mobile Municipal Archives, Mobile, Alabama.

3. Ralph Dennis Metzger, "History of the Mobile Air Service Command: First Installment—Mobile Air Depot: January 1939–February 1943," 27–33. This unpublished official history is deposited at the Mobile Municipal Archives.

4. *Brookley Bay Breeze,* Mar. 6, Apr. 10, Sept. 13, 1943; *A la Moad,* July 5, 1943.

5. *Brookley Bay Breeze,* Mar. 27, 1943; *A la Moad,* May 24, July 5, 1943.

6. *A la Moad,* June 14, July 7, 1943.

7. *Mobile Press Register,* Sept. 27, 1942; *A la Moad,* July 5, 1943.

8. Metzger, "History of the Mobile Air Service Command," 31–32;

Brookley Bay Breeze, May 10, 1942, Apr. 10, 1943; *Mobile Press Register,* Sept. 27, 1942.

9. *Welfarer,* June 18, 1944. This publication is the third newsletter published by MoASC and is deposited at the Mobile Municipal Archives.

10. Margaret Davis Frazier to Civil Service Department, Apr. 1, 1943; Zemma D. Camphor to U.S. Civil Service Board, Aug. 27, 1943, FEPC Records, RG 228, Box 753, Atlanta Branch, NA; Comments of Workers on Specified Items—Mobile, Alabama, 1944, Women's Bureau, RG 86, NA.

11. *A la Moad,* Feb. 28, 1944; *Welfarer,* Feb. 18, Dec. 3, 1945.

12. "Labor Market Developments Reports for the Mobile Area," June 12, 1943, July 1944, Nov. 1944, Bureau of Employment Security, RG 183, Box 3, NA.

13. *Mobile Press Register,* Sept. 13, 1942; "Labor Market Developments Report for the Mobile Area," Oct. 28, 1942, June 12, 1943, Bureau of Employment Security, RG 183, Box 3, NA.

14. *Fore & Aft,* July 6, 1945. This newsletter published by ADDSCO during the war is deposited at the City of Mobile Museum.

15. *Fore & Aft,* Mar. 16, July 6, 1944.

16. Ibid., July 28, 1944.

17. Ibid., Feb. 4, Mar. 3, 10, 17, Apr. 21, July 28, Aug. 25, Sept. 8, 15, 22, Oct. 3, 13, 20, 1944, Jan. 4, Mar. 23, June 29, July 27, 1945; *Mobile Press Register,* Mar. 7, 1943.

18. Margaret Bernard to President Roosevelt, Apr. 17, 1944, FEPC Records, RG 228, Box 793, Atlanta Branch, NA; Comments of Workers on Specific Items—Mobile, Alabama, 1944.

19. *Birmingham News,* Nov. 14, 15, 1942, Feb. 13, 1943.

20. "Labor Market Developments Report for Birmingham," June 1, Sept. 27, 1943, Bureau of Employment Security, RG 183, Box 1, NA.

21. *Birmingham News,* July 11, 21, 30, Aug. 4, 15, 1943, Sept. 9, 1944; "Demand-Supply Supplement for Birmingham," Mar. 1944, Sept. 1944, Bureau of Employment Security, RG 183, Box 1, NA.

22. Martha Riley to A. Bruce Hunt, Feb. 17, 1944, FEPC Records, RG 228, Box 760, Atlanta Branch, NA; Mary B. Summers to President Roosevelt, Feb. 22, 1944, ibid., Box 764; *Birmingham World,* July 13, 1943; Memorandum from WMC to Birmingham USES, FEPC Records, RG 228, Box 750, Atlanta branch, NA.

23. Alabama Department of Industrial Relations, "Survey of the Employment Situation in the Childersburg, Alabama Area," Dec. 15, 1941, Bureau of Employment Security, RG 183, Box 2, NA; "Labor Market Developments Reports for Talladega," Apr. 2, June 12, Aug. 8, Oct. 10, 1943, ibid., Box

4; "Talladega Demand-Supply Supplement," May 1944, Sept. 1944, ibid., Box 5.

24. *Birmingham World,* June 22, 1943; FEPC Final Disposition Report, Case no. 7-GR-221, May 23, 1945, FEPC Records, RG 228, Box 760, Atlanta Branch, NA; Evelyn Keith to George M. Johnson, Jan. 7, 1944, ibid., Box 764.

25. "Labor Market Developments Report for Huntsville," Aug. 9, Oct. 7, Dec. 4, 1943, Bureau of Employment Security, RG 183, Box 2, NA; *Birmingham News,* July 7, 1943.

26. "Labor Market Developments Report for Talladega," Aug. 8, 1943, Bureau of Employment Security, RG 183, Box 5, NA; "Labor Market Developments Report for Anniston," Aug. 9, 1943, ibid., Box 1; "Labor Market Developments Report for Gadsden," June 14, 1943, ibid., Box 2; "Labor Market Developments Report for Decatur," Aug. 11, 1943, ibid.

27. *Montgomery Advertiser,* June 15, 1941; *Birmingham News,* June 6, Dec. 14, 1942, Jan. 1, 14, 31, Feb. 18, July 21, Aug. 2, Nov. 7, 14, 1943.

28. *Birmingham World,* Feb. 2, Apr. 9, 1943.

29. Ibid., Oct. 9, 1942, Feb. 12, 19, Mar. 5, Apr. 23, July 23, Sept. 6, 1943; Karen Tucker Anderson, "Last Hired, First Fired: Black Women Workers during World War II," *Journal of American History* 69 (June 1982): 92–93.

30. U.S. Department of Labor, Women's Bureau, Bulletin 209, *Women Workers in Ten War Production Areas and Their Postwar Employment Plans* (Washington, D.C.: U.S. Government Printing Office, 1946).

31. Susan Hartmann, *The Home Front and Beyond: American Women in the 1940s* (Boston: G. K. Hall/Twayne, 1982), 80; Anderson, "Last Hired, First Fired," 92–93.

32. Anniston Warehouse File, Box 748, FEPC Records, RG 228, Atlanta Branch, NA.

33. *Birmingham News,* Jan. 24, Oct. 10, 1943. Hallie Farmer, professor of history and government at Alabama College for Women (University of Montevallo) described the Alabama home front at this conference. She had recently edited the series of essays *War Comes to Alabama,* as well as having written the concluding article on postwar prospects.

34. Leila Rupp, *Mobilizing Women for War: German and American Propaganda, 1939–1945* (Princeton: Princeton University Press, 1978), 165.

35. *Fore & Aft,* June 9, Aug. 25, Sept. 1, 22, 1944, Jan. 5, 12, Feb. 9, Apr. 27, June 22, 1945; *Brookley Bay Breeze,* Apr. 24, 1943; *A la Moad,* Sept. 13, 29, 1943; *Welfarer,* May 18, June 18, Sept. 3, 1945.

36. *Welfarer,* Jan. 3, 1945.

37. D'Ann Campbell, *Women at War with America: Private Lives in a Public Era* (Cambridge; Mass.: Harvard University Press, 1984), 72–73.

38. *A la Moad,* Nov. 8, Sept. 27, 1943; *Welfarer,* Apr. 18, 1945.

39. *A la Moad,* Sept. 13, 29, July 26, 1943.

40. *Welfarer,* Sept. 18, 1944, Mar. 3, 1945; *A la Moad,* Feb. 28, 1944.

41. *Welfarer,* Sept. 3, 1944, Jan. 1, 1945.

42. Ibid., July 18, 1944; *A la Moad,* Jan. 1, 31, 1944.

Chapter 4

1. Susan Hartmann, *The Home Front and Beyond: American Women in the 1940s* (Boston: G. K. Hall/Twayne, 1982), 60–61.

2. *Fore & Aft,* Jan. 1, Sept. 8, Nov. 3, 1944, Jan. 5, Apr. 6, 1945; *A la Moad,* Feb. 21, 1944.

3. *Mobile Register,* Feb. 2, 1944.

4. *Fore & Aft,* Jan. 21, Feb. 4, 25, Mar. 3, Aug. 4, 1944.

5. *Birmingham News,* July 2, 1942.

6. *Mobile Press Register,* Apr. 18, 1943.

7. Ibid., Apr. 18, 1945, Feb. 13, 1944; "Labor Market Developments Reports for Mobile," June 12, 1943, Bureau of Employment Security, RG 185, Box 3, NA; *Brookley Bay Breeze,* Apr. 3, 1943.

8. Nancy Woloch, *Women and the American Experience* (New York: Alfred A. Knopf, 1984), 465; William H. Chafe, *The American Woman: Her Changing Social, Economic, and Political Roles, 1920–1970* (New York: Oxford University Press, 1972), 165–73.

9. "Day Care for Children of Employed Mothers," *Alabama Social Welfare,* May 1942, p. 7.

10. "The Relationship of ADC Grants to the Employment of Women," *Alabama Social Welfare,* June 1942, p. 12; "Day Care Facilities to Meet the Needs of Children," ibid., Aug. 1942, p. 9.

11. "Relationship of ADC Grants to the Employment of Women," 12; "Day Care Facilities to Meet the Needs of Children," 9; "Community Planning for the Care of Children of Employed Mothers," *Alabama Social Welfare,* Oct. 1942, pp. 10–12.

12. "Day Care for Children of Employed Mothers," 7–8.

13. War Manpower Commission, "Proposed Manpower Program for the Mobile Area," Aug. 4, 1943, Bureau of Employment Security, RG 183, Box 3, NA.

14. *Mobile Press Register,* Oct. 25, 1942; "Resurvey of Employment

Situation in Mobile," Sept. 29, 1942, Bureau of Employment Security, RG 183, Box 3, NA; "Labor Market Developments Report for Mobile," June 12, 1943, ibid.

15. *Mobile Press Register,* July 4, 1943; "Congested Production Area Report," Nov. 30, 1943, Bureau of Employment Security, RG 183, Box 3, NA; *Mobile Register,* June 9, 1943; *Fore & Aft,* June 23, 1944.

16. *Mobile Register,* June 9, Aug. 1, 28, Oct. 10, 1943.

17. *Birmingham News,* Mar. 19, May 4, 1943; "What a Day Care Center Does in a War Area," *Alabama Social Welfare,* Apr. 1943, pp. 6–7.

18. "Congested Production Area Report," Nov. 30, 1943; "Congestion Production Area Report," Oct. 14, 1944, Bureau of Employment Security, RG 183, Box 3, NA.

19. *Mobile Press Register,* June 20, July 4, Aug. 1, 1943.

20. "Labor Market Developments Report," June 12, 1943; Hartmann, *The Home Front and Beyond,* 85.

21. *Mobile Register,* Nov. 23, 1942.

22. "Mothers in Industry," *Alabama Social Welfare,* Sept. 1943, p. 11.

23. *Birmingham News,* June 2, 1943.

24. Ibid., Aug. 31, 1943.

25. *Mobile Press Register,* Jan. 3, 1943; *Mobile Register,* Jan. 22, Oct. 11, 1943.

26. *Mobile Register,* Apr. 15, 16, 23, 1943.

27. Ibid., Apr. 15, 1943; "Defense Developments in Alabama," Department of Public Welfare, Montgomery, Alabama, Aug. 1, 1941, Department of Archives and History, Montgomery; "Juvenile Delinquency in Montgomery," *Alabama Social Welfare,* Apr. 1943, p. 7.

28. "Labor Market Developments Report for the Mobile Area," Oct. 28, 1942, June 12, 1943, Bureau of Employment Security, RG 183, Box 3, NA.

29. Melton McLaurin and Michael Thomason, *Mobile: The Life and Times of a Great Southern City* (Woodland Hills, Calif.: Windsor Publications, 1981); *Mobile Register,* Apr. 14, 1943.

30. *Mobile Register,* Jan. 19, 1944.

31. Ibid., Apr. 23, 1943.

32. *Mobile Press Register,* July 4, Dec. 5, 1943.

33. Hartmann, *The Home Front and Beyond,* 66–70.

34. Woloch, *Women and the American Experience,* 469; Chafe, *American Woman,* 174–81.

35. "Labor Market Developments Report for Mobile," July 1945, Program and Action Table I, Bureau of Employment Security, RG 183, Box 3, NA; "Labor Market Developments Report for Mobile," May 1946, ibid.

36. *Fore & Aft,* July 6, Mar. 16, 1945.

37. "Labor Market Developments Report for Mobile," July 1945, Table I; "Labor Market Developments Report for Mobile," May 1946; "Labor Market Developments Report for Mobile," Nov. 1946, Bureau of Employment Security, RG 183, Box 3, NA.

38. "Labor Market Developments Report for Birmingham," Aug. 1945, ibid., Box 1.

39. Theresa Wolfson, "Aprons and Overalls in the War," *Annals of the American Academy of Political and Social Science* 229 (Sept. 1943): 56–63; Susan Estabrook Kennedy, *If All We Did Was to Weep at Home: A History of White Working-Class Women in America* (Bloomington: Indiana University Press, 1979), 199.

40. *Welfarer,* July 18, Sept. 3, 18, 1944.

41. Ibid., Sept. 18, 1944.

42. *A la Moad,* Apr. 3, 1944, Dec. 13, 1944; *Welfarer,* Sept. 18, Mar. 18, 1943, Apr. 3, Feb. 3, 1945.

43. Hartmann, *The Home Front and Beyond,* 90.

44. Karen Anderson, *Wartime Women: Sex Roles, Family Relations, and the Status of Women during World War II* (Westport, Conn.: Greenwood Press, 1981), 163.

45. U.S. Department of Labor, Women's Bureau, Bulletin 209, *Women Workers in Ten War Production Areas and Their Postwar Employment Plans* (Washington, D.C.: U.S. Government Printing Office, 1946).

Chapter 5

1. Richard Polenberg, *War and Society: The United States, 1941–1945* (Philadelphia: Lippincott, 1972), 131–53; Richard R. Lingeman, *Don't You Know There's a War On? The American Home Front, 1941–1945* (New York: Putnam's, 1970), 65–110.

2. D'Ann Campbell, *Women at War with America: Private Lives in a Public Era* (Cambridge, Mass.: Harvard University Press, 1984), 66–67.

3. Lingeman, *Don't You Know There's a War On?* 25–35.

4. *Birmingham News,* Nov. 26, 1946; *Home Front* (Alabama State Defense Council, Montgomery, Ala.), June 1944. *Home Front* is deposited at the Department of Archives and History in Montgomery, Alabama.

5. *Montgomery Advertiser,* May 28, 1942; *Birmingham News,* Feb. 11, 1943; "Volunteers and the Civilian Defense Program," *Alabama Social Welfare,* Aug. 1942, pp. 7–9; *Home Front,* Oct. 1944.

6. *Birmingham News,* Aug. 4, 1942, Apr. 5, 1943; Lingeman, *Don't You Know There's a War On?* 61; *Birmingham World,* Mar. 20, 1942.

7. *Birmingham News,* Aug. 2, 9, 1942; "Civilian Defense in Montgomery County," *Alabama Social Welfare,* Jan. 1943, pp. 3–5.

8. *Birmingham News,* July 30, 1942.

9. Lingeman, *Don't You Know There's a War On?* 51–52.

10. *Mobile Press Register,* Sept. 4, 1942, Jan. 1, 1943; *Mobile Register,* July 4, 18, 25, 1943.

11. "Volunteers and the Civilian Defense Program"; "Community Wartime Services," *Alabama Social Welfare,* Dec. 1942, pp. 2–3.

12. "Civilian Defense in Montgomery County."

13. *Birmingham News,* June 23, 25, 30, 1943.

14. *Birmingham News,* Sept. 5, 1943.

15. *Mobile Register,* Feb. 28, 1943; *Birmingham News,* Jan. 9, 1944; *Birmingham World,* Mar. 20, June 11, 1943; *Mobile Weekly Advocate,* Mar. 20, 1943.

16. *Mobile Register,* Sept. 27, 1942, June 6, 13, 15, July 9, Nov. 14, 22, 29, 1943, Jan. 2, 1944; *Birmingham News,* July 26, 1942, Feb. 14, 1943.

17. *Mobile Press Register,* Nov. 8, 1942.

18. *Birmingham News,* Aug. 2, 1943, Apr. 4, May 19, 1943; *Mobile Press Register,* Feb. 28, 1943, Jan. 30, 1944; *A la Moad,* Sept. 13, 1943; Campbell, *Women at War with America,* 69.

19. Interview with Julia R. Walpole conducted by Paul A. Breck, Jan. 25, 1980, Department of Archives, Birmingham Public Library, Birmingham, Alabama; *Birmingham News,* Dec. 28, 1941, Sept. 12, 1943.

20. Interview with Julia R. Walpole.

21. *Birmingham World,* Feb. 13, 27, 1942, Feb. 2, 1943; *Alabama Citizen and the Tuscaloosa Weekly Review,* Dec. 23, 1944; interview with Julia R. Walpole.

22. Lingeman, *Don't You Know There's a War On?* 249; *Birmingham News,* Nov. 2, Dec. 1, 3, 1942.

23. *Birmingham News,* Aug. 14, 16, 1942.

24. Lingeman, *Don't You Know There's a War On?* 266–67.

25. *Birmingham News,* Feb. 11, 18, 1943; *Birmingham World,* Apr. 2, 1943.

26. *Birmingham News,* Feb. 13, 1943.

27. *Mobile Press Register,* July 4, Sept. 5, 1943; *Birmingham News,* Oct. 22, 24, 1943.

Chapter 6

1. Campbell, *Women at War with America: Private Lives in a Public Era* (Cambridge, Mass.: Harvard University Press, 1984), 165.

2. Richard R. Lingeman, *Don't You Know There's a War On?* *The American Home Front, 1941–1945* (New York: Putnam's, 1970), 258.

3. *Alabama Citizen and the Tuscaloosa Weekly Review,* Feb. 10, 1945; *Birmingham News,* Jan. 1, 1943.

4. *Mobile Press Register,* Nov. 29, 1942; *Mobile Register,* June 21, 1943.

5. *Birmingham World,* Jan. 29, 1943. These "Eleanor Clubs" were named for Eleanor Roosevelt, who supported the rights of blacks.

7. *Birmingham News,* Jan. 5, Feb. 19, May 28, 1943; *Birmingham World,* May 4, 1943.

8. *Birmingham World,* Apr. 2, 23, 1943.

9. *Birmingham News,* Feb. 7, 1943.

10. *Mobile Press,* Nov. 7, 1942; *Birmingham News,* Feb. 7, 1943; Lingeman, *Don't You Know There's a War On?* 255.

11. *Mobile Press Register,* Nov. 29, 1942; *Mobile Register,* Jan. 15, 16, 1943.

12. *Mobile Register,* May 21, Nov. 23, 1943.

13. *Birmingham News,* June 14, 25, 1942, Mar. 24, Apr. 6, 9, June 3, 15, 1943; *Mobile Register,* Feb. 17, 1943; *Birmingham World,* Feb. 22, 1942.

14. John Dos Passos, *State of the Nation* (Boston: Houghton Mifflin, 1944), 92–93.

15. *Mobile Weekly Advocate,* Aug. 8, 1942.

16. "Labor Market Developments Report for Talladega," Dec. 10, 1943, Bureau of Employment Security, RG 183, Box 5, NA.

17. *Huntsville Times,* Oct. 23, 30, Nov. 30, 1941; *Birmingham News,* Apr. 25, 1943; "National Defense Migration in the Southeast," *Alabama Social Welfare,* June 1942.

18. *Birmingham News,* July 27, Dec. 6, 1942; *Mobile Register,* Aug. 3, Sept. 27, Oct. 12, 1943; Melton McLaurin and Michael Thomason, *The Life and Times of a Great Southern City* (Woodland Hills, Calif.: Windsor Publications, 1981), 126.

19. *Mobile Register,* Aug. 3, Sept. 27, Oct. 12, 1943.

20. *Birmingham News,* Aug. 2, 23, Dec. 27, 1942, Jan. 24, 1943.

21. "Labor Market Developments Report for Gadsden," Apr. 15, 1943, Bureau of Employment Security, RG 183, Box 2, NA; *Birmingham News,* Feb. 14, 1943.

22. "Survey of the Employment Situation in the Childersburg, Alabama, Area," Dec. 15, 1941, Bureau of Employment Security, RG 183, Box 2, NA; "Labor Market Developments Report for Talladega," Dec. 10, 1943.

23. *Birmingham World,* Jan. 30, Feb. 27, 1942.

24. *Mobile Register,* Aug. 29, Sept. 18, 1942; Agnes E. Meyer, *Journey through Chaos* (New York: Harcourt, Brace and Co., 1943), 202–13; *Mobile*

Register, June 24, Aug. 3, 13, 1943; *Mobile Press Register,* July 18, 25, 1943, Mar. 5, 1944.

25. *Mobile Register,* Mar. 9, 1944, Sept. 3, 1943; Meyer, *Journey through Chaos,* 204.

26. *Mobile Register,* Dec. 14, 1943.

27. Ibid., Sept. 7, 8, Dec. 14, 1943, Jan. 1, 8, 1944.

28. *Mobile Press Register,* Feb. 13, 1944; *Mobile Register,* Feb. 22, 1944.

29. *Mobile Register,* Feb. 12, 13, 1944.

30. *Mobile Press Register,* Feb. 20, 1944; *Mobile Press,* Feb. 22, 1944; *Mobile Register,* Feb. 25, 1944.

Conclusion

1. Susan Hartmann, *The Home Front and Beyond: American Women in the 1940s* (Boston: G. K. Hall/Twayne, 1982), 77–78.

2. U.S. Department of Commerce, Bureau of the Census, *Characteristics of the Population, Labor Force, Families and Housing, Mobile Congested Production Area, March 1944* (Washington, D.C.: U.S. Government Printing Office, 1944), Table 10.

3. Ibid.

4. Ibid., Table 5.

5. Ibid.

6. U.S. Department of Labor, Women's Bureau, Bulletin 209, *Women Workers in Ten War Production Areas and Their Postwar Employment Plans* (Washington, D.C.: U.S. Government Printing Office, 1946).

7. Ibid.

8. *Birmingham News,* July 7, 1943; *Mobile Press Register,* Sept. 13, 1942.

9. "The Child Welfare Program of the American Legion in Action," *Alabama Social Welfare,* July 1944, pp. 2–3.

10. *Birmingham News,* June 2, 1943; *Anniston Star,* Feb. 21, 1945.

11. U.S. Department of Commerce, Bureau of the Census, *Census of Population: 1950,* Vol. 2, *Characteristics of the Population* (Washington, D.C.: U.S. Government Printing Office, 1952), Part 2, Alabama, pp. 41–42.

12. Ibid., 40–42.

13. Ibid., 41–42.

14. Ibid., 40.

15. Interview with Elizabeth Sisson, Jefferson County, Alabama, Office

of Senior Citizens' Activities, Program on Working Women, 1977, Department of Archives, Birmingham Public Library, Birmingham, Alabama.

16. Interviews with Mayme Kirby, Mary Stinson, and Elizabeth Sisson, ibid.

17. "War Services Report VI," *Alabama Social Welfare,* Nov. 1943, pp. 3–11; "War Services Report VII," *Alabama Social Welfare,* Feb. 1944, pp. 7–13.

Essay on

Sources

The major manuscript sources used in this study were U.S. government records, most of which are located in the National Archives in Washington, D.C. Because Mobile was one of the ten most congested areas during the war, many government records dealt specifically with the city as well as the state. The most useful government records were those relating to the Bureau of Employment Security, Women's Bureau, War Manpower Commission, Committee for Congested Production Areas, Bureau of the Census, Office of War Information, Office of Community War Services, and Committee on Post-War Employment Problems. The records of the President's Fair Employment Practices Committee, located in the Atlanta branch of the National Archives, were a valuable source of information on black women's experience.

Manuscripts pertaining to the history of the state of Alabama are located at the Department of Archives and History in Montgomery, the City of Mobile Museum, the Mobile Municipal Archives, the Mobile Public Library, and the Department of Archives of the Birmingham Public Library. Among the most useful sources in the State Department of Archives was *Alabama Social Welfare*, a journal published by the State Department of Public Welfare during the 1930s and 1940s. Also in the archives is *Home Front*, a monthly bulletin of the Alabama State Defense Council; "Defense Developments in Alabama," a manuscript of the Department of Public Welfare; and the papers of the wartime governors, Chauncey Sparks and Frank Dixon. The Mobile Municipal Archives has the three invaluable newsletters of the Mobile Air Service Command, *Brookley Bay Breeze, A la Moad,* and the *Welfarer,* and the "History of the Mobile Air Service Command," an official unpublished study by Ralph Dennis Metzger. The newsletter of the Alabama Dry Dock and Shipbuilding Company, *Fore & Aft,* is deposited at the City of Mobile Museum. A movie made by the Office of War Information in 1943 about Mobile entitled *War Town* can be found at the Mobile Public Library. The Department of Archives of the Birmingham Public Library has several very useful oral interviews with World War II women. The Office of Senior Citizens' Activities of Jefferson County conducted a series of oral interviews with working women, some of whom were employed during the war. The archives also has an oral interview with Julia R. Walpole, who was a major leader in the Birmingham USO.

Since very little has been written about the history of Alabama after the 1940s, historians must rely heavily upon newspapers of the state. Extensive use was made of the *Mobile Press,* the *Mobile Register,* the *Birmingham News,* the *Montgomery Advertiser,* the *Huntsville Times,* the *Anniston Star,* and the *Talladega News.* The most useful black newspaper was the *Birmingham World.* Other black papers are the *Baptist Leader,* the *Mobile Weekly Advocate,* and the *Alabama Citizen and the Tuscaloosa Weekly Review,* all of which are located at the state archives. A Ph.D. dissertation by Bernadette Loftin, "A Social History of the Mid-Gulf South: Panama City to Mobile, 1930–1950," written in 1971 at the University of Southern Mississippi, is the best work available on Mobile during the war. Edward L. Ullman's dissertation, "Mobile: Industrial Seaport and Trade Center" (University of Chicago, 1943), is an excellent survey of the city's economy on the eve of World War II.

Even though women's history is a relatively new field, much attention has been given to the World War II period. William H. Chafe wrote the first serious work on women after 1920, *The American Woman: Her Changing Social, Economic, and Political Roles, 1920–1970* (New York: Oxford University Press, 1972). Leila Rupp has written an excellent comparative study, *Mobilizing Women for War: German and American Propaganda, 1939–1945* (Princeton: Princeton University Press, 1978). Karen Anderson in *Wartime Women: Sex Roles, Family Relations, and the Status of Women during World War II* (Westport, Conn.: Greenwood Press, 1981) dealt with the production centers of Baltimore, Detroit, and Seattle. She discussed women's family roles as well as their work roles. Eleanor Straub investigated women's exclusion from the decision-making process in the recruitment drives at the national level in her article "United States Government Policy toward Civilian Women during World War II," *Prologue* 5 (Winter 1973): 240–54, and her dissertation, "Government Policy toward Civilian Women during World War II" (Emory University, 1973). Susan Hartmann in *The Home Front and Beyond: American Women in the 1940s* (Boston: G. K. Hall/Twayne, 1982) provided a masterful analysis of the role of women not only during the war years but also in the immediate postwar period in the areas of education, law, and politics. D'Ann Campbell in *Women at War with America: Private Lives in a Public Era* (Cambridge, Mass.: Harvard University Press, 1984) explored all the major roles of women during the war in the military, in nursing, in factories, in volunteer work, and in the home. Maureen Honey's *Creating Rosie the Riveter: Class, Gender, and Propaganda during World War II* (Amherst: University of Massachusetts Press, 1984) is concerned with the question why the changed media image of women failed to survive the war.

Several recent works provided background for the war years by analyzing the preceding decade. The most useful are Susan Ware, *Beyond Suffrage: Women in the New Deal* (Cambridge, Mass.: Harvard University Press, 1981); Lois Scharf, *To Work and to Wed: Female Employment, Feminism, and the Great Depression* (Westport, Conn.: Greenwood Press, 1980); and Winifred D. Wandersee, *Women's Work and Family Values, 1920–1940* (Cambridge, Mass.: Harvard University Press, 1981).

The role of working women has been the subject of an increasing number of historians' investigations. Several of these include substantial coverage of the expansion of the labor force during the war: Alice Kessler-Harris, *Out to Work: A History of Wage-Earning Women in the United States* (New York: Oxford University Press, 1982); Susan Estabrook Kennedy, *If All We Did Was to Weep at Home: A History of White Working-Class Women in America* (Bloomington: Indiana University Press, 1979); and Rosalyn Baxandall, Linda Gordon, and Susan Reverby, eds., *America's Working Women* (New York: Vintage Books, 1976).

Several recent histories of the home front have added to our understanding of the society of the war period. The most useful of these are Richard R. Lingeman, *Don't You Know There's a War On? The American Home Front, 1941–1945* (New York: Putnam's, 1970); Richard Polenberg, *War and Society: The United States, 1941–1945* (Philadelphia: J. B. Lippincott Co., 1972); and George Q. Flynn, *The Mess in Washington: Manpower Mobilization in World War II* (Westport, Conn.: Greenwood Press, 1979). A work written immediately after the war is Jack Goodman, ed., *While You Were Gone: A Report on Wartime Life in the United States* (New York: Simon and Schuster, 1946), which is a series of essays by contemporaries.

Two other contemporary accounts that devote large sections to Mobile are Agnes E. Meyer, *Journey Through Chaos* (New York: Harcourt, Brace and Co., 1943), and John Dos Passos, *State of the Nation* (Boston: Houghton Mifflin, 1944).

Among the few secondary accounts dealing with the South and Alabama, George Brown Tindall's massive work, *The Emergence of the New South,*

1913–1945 (Baton Rouge: Louisiana State University Press, 1967), has a concluding chapter covering the war years. Two illustrated histories of Mobile and Birmingham cover portions of the war period. Melton McLaurin and Michael Thomason's *Mobile: The Life and Times of a Great Southern City* (Woodland Hills, Calif.: Windsor Publications, 1981) has an excellent brief description of the changes experienced by Mobile during the 1940s. The second is Leah Rawls Atkins's *The Valley and the Hills: An Illustrated History of Birmingham and Jefferson County* (Woodland Hills, Calif.: Windsor Publications, 1981). The University of Alabama put together in *War Comes to Alabama* (University, Ala.: University of Alabama, 1943) a series of essays by various state officials describing the effect of the war on the state. Nearly all expressed fear that the boom years would not last and a depression would follow the war.

Index

ADDSCO. *See* Alabama Dry Dock and
  Shipbuilding Company
Aircraft modification, 7, 11, 36. *See also*
  Betchel-McCone-Parsons Company
Aircraft repair, 24, 36, 38. *See also*
  Mobile Air Service Command
Air raids, mock, 84–85
Alabama Dry Dock and Shipbuilding
  Company (ADDSCO), 9, 58, 63, 65,
  116, 118; recruitment drive, 22–24;
  working conditions, 24; employment
  of women, 41–45; layoffs at war's
  end, 77
Alabama Ordnance Works, 8, 15, 118;
  employment in, 48–49
Alabama Polytechnic Institute, 33, 47
Alabama Social Welfare, 69, 124 (n. 24)
Alabama State Advisory Committee on
  Day Care, 68, 69
Alabama State Defense Council, 84
Alabama State Department of Public
  Welfare, 68
ALCOA, 11
Anderson, Karen, 2
Anderson, Mary, 7, 23, 67
Anniston, Ala., 8, 9, 11; description of
  wartime conditions, 16–17
Anniston Army Depot, 11, 16–17, 53
Army Air Forces Aircraft Warning
  Service, 86

Army Air Forces Basic Flying School,
  11, 93
Arsenals. *See* Ordnance plants
Atmore, 104
Auburn University. *See* Alabama Poly-
  technic Institute

Bancroft, Bill, 93
Bechtel-McCone-Parsons Company, 8,
  10, 106, 118; training programs, 34;
  description of female employment,
  45–48; investigated by federal government, 47; layoffs at war's end, 78
Birmingham, 8, 9, 10, 36, 78, 85, 97,
  99, 105, 106; increase in population,
  14; description of wartime conditions,
  14–15; recruitment drive, 22; training
  programs, 32–33; survey by Chamber
  of Commerce, 45; extended shopping
  hours, 66; child care facilities, 71;
  concern with juvenile delinquency,
  73; civilian defense, 84–85; Citizens'
  Service Corps, 87; nurses' aides,
  90; Red Cross, 91; housing shortages,
  106; crowded schools, 108
Birmingham News, 33, 97, 101
Birmingham-Southern College, 33
Birmingham World, 34, 38, 51, 93
Black colleges, 33. *See also* Tuskegee
  Institute

141

About the Author

Mary Martha Thomas is professor of history at Jacksonville State University. She received her doctorate from Emory University, her master's degree from the University of Michigan, and her bachelor's from Southern Methodist University. She is the author of *Southern Methodist University: Founding and Early Years* (1974).